About Island Press

Since 1984, the nonprofit organization Island Press has been stim-ulating, shaping, and communicating ideas that are essential for solving environmental problems worldwide. With more than 1,000 titles in print and some 30 new releases each year, we are the nation's leading publisher on environmental issues. We identify innovative thinkers and emerging trends in the environmental field. We work with world-renowned experts and authors to develop cross-disciplinary solutions to environmental challenges.

Island Press designs and executes educational campaigns, in conjunction with our authors, to communicate their critical mes-sages in print, in person, and online using the latest technologies, innovative programs, and the media. Our goal is to reach targeted audiences—scientists, policy makers, environmental advocates, urban planners, the media, and concerned citizens—with infor-mation that can be used to create the framework for long-term ecological health and human well-being.

Island Press gratefully acknowledges major support from The Bobolink Foundation, Caldera Foundation, The Curtis and Edith Munson Foundation, The Forrest C. and Frances H. Lattner Foundation, The JPB Foundation, The Kresge Foundation, The Summit Charitable Foundation, Inc., and many other generous organizations and indi-viduals.

The opinions expressed in this book are those of the author(s) and do not necessarily reflect the views of our supporters.

BETTER BUSES,
BETTER CITIES

BETTER BUSES, BETTER CITIES

How to Plan, Run, and Win the Fight for Effective Transit

STEVEN HIGASHIDE

ISLANDPRESS   Washington | Covelo | London

ISLAND PRESS is a trademark of the Center for Resource Economics.

Library of Congress Control Number: 2019938723

All Island Press books are printed on environmentally responsible materials.

Manufactured in the United States of America
10 9 8 7 6 5 4 3

Keywords
autonomous vehicle, bus operator, bus rapid transit (BRT), bus shelter, captive rider, choice rider, equity, fair fares, microtransit, National Association of City Transportation Officials (NACTO), public transit, TransitCenter, transportation funding, transportation planning, transportation policy, transportation technology, walkability

CONTENTS

—

PREFACE

—

My Own Bus Story

As a public transportation researcher and advocate, I've heard a lot of personal stories about the bus. Some of these came during focus groups of transit riders I've organized as part of my work. Other stories have come from the public servants working to deliver better bus service and the activists and elected officials working to win it from the outside. This book shares the stories of dozens of people, across the country, working to make bus service better. It seems only right that I share my own story as well.

Riding the bus figures into my earliest memories, of taking a Chicago Transit Authority crosstown local to the beaches of Lake Michigan with my family. Memory is a malleable thing, and I can't fully trust in my recollection of the vehicle's white, blue, and red livery; the blue fabric-backed seats; the plastic shovels and castle molds I carried in a mesh bag. But I know the bus made my childhood meaningfully richer.

After my family moved to the suburbs of New Jersey, I didn't take a public bus again until high school, when my friends and I visited Manhattan. Like many people, I mostly found buses confusing but easy to ignore. How buses worked was secret knowledge, written down in obscure pamphlets I never tried to track down.

That changed when I spent a college semester in London. By 2006, London was in the midst of an incredible transformation of its transportation network. Three years earlier, the city had introduced a "congestion charge," tolling private vehicles entering busy central neighborhoods. It vastly expanded its bus network to prepare for the change and carpeted its streets with miles of red bus-only lanes. The buses were fast, cruising past lines of taxis and trucks. They were easy to use, with a quick tap of the "Oyster" smartcard granting access. They felt ubiquitous, arriving often and seemingly going to every place. Even then, before I knew I would make transportation a career, I found this revelatory.

I fell for transit while interning at a nonprofit advocacy group, the Tri-State Transportation Campaign, based in New York City. My first accomplishment was writing a report on how better bus service could help people in New York's Hudson Valley. At Tri-State, I realized that the deepest expertise sometimes resides outside of government and the media and that change is often impossible without outside agitation. It was there that I first learned how to craft a sound bite, endure angry phone calls from officials I had criticized, and lurk in the hallways to catch lawmakers on their way to vote. I helped pass legislation protecting transit funding in Connecticut, defended transportation reformers in New York City government from criticism, and killed congressional attempts to defund transit.

Most recently, I've directed research efforts at TransitCenter, a foundation that works to improve transit in the United States by conducting research, supporting advocacy campaigns, and convening transit reformers. I've authored and commissioned research into what transit riders want, how demographics influence transit ridership, how parking rules and federal tax policy change how we get around, and what city leaders should do to create great transportation systems. Best of all, I've gotten to meet and learn from hundreds of people working to change public transit in this country.

I believe we need a bigger, broader transit reform movement in America. For this book, I was lucky to speak with dozens of people who are part of that movement today: advocates, elected leaders, researchers, transportation professionals, and philanthropists. I want to acknowledge that many of them are colleagues; some work with organizations that TransitCenter has supported through grants. Unlike the book that some journalists and researchers might write, this is not a dispassionate analysis, done at remove. It is an opinionated argument for better buses in our cities, drawing on the latest transportation research, my own work, and the experiences of many people working to make their own communities better places to live.

ACKNOWLEDGMENTS

—

Writing this book was like taking the bus in a new city, with detours and missed stops and plenty of pauses along the way to reorient myself. I was lucky to have the guidance of a steady and patient editor, Heather Boyer, who encouraged and coached me through the toughest spots and kept me on board.

I would never have been in the position to write this book were it not for all I've learned from fellow activists, journalists, researchers, and practitioners. Among them, I'd especially like to thank my current and former colleagues at TransitCenter, including David Bragdon, Tabitha Decker, Mary Buchanan, Rosalie Ray, Kirk Hovenkotter, Hayley Richardson, Jennifer Elam, Chris Pangilinan, Stephanie Lotshaw, Zak Accuardi, Jon Orcutt, Joelle Ballam-Schwan, Julia Ehrman, and Shin-pei Tsay.

I'm grateful to everyone who took the time to speak on the record with me for this project: Nicole Barnes, Simon Berrebi, Bill Bryant, Azhar Chougle, Cheryl Cort, Aimee Custis, Berry Farrington, Mark Fisher, Shawn Fleek, Lisa Jacobson, Megan Kanagy, Patrick Kennedy, Irin Limargo, Orlando Lopez, Kurt Luhrsen, Beth Osborne, Annise Parker, Mary Skelton Roberts, Caitlin Schwartz, Joshua Sikich, Christof Spieler, Stacy Thompson, Marta Viciedo, Jarrett Walker, and Sam Zimbabwe. And thanks to the many other reformers planning, running, and fighting for effective and equitable transit around the country.

Chad Frischmann of Project Drawdown helped me understand their climate mitigation modeling. TransitCenter, the National Association of City Transportation Officials, the Barr Foundation, Outfront/Decaux, J. Daniel Malouff, OPAL, and Jarrett Walker graciously provided images.

Hayley Richardson deserves a second mention. Your belief inspired me to set off on the journey of writing this book. Your love, support, and counsel were essential to my seeing it through. On to the next adventure!

INTRODUCTION

We Need to Unleash the Bus

Most of what we hear about the bus in the United States is demoralizing.

It's true in journalism. In 2014, a team of student reporters collaborated on the "Connecticut Bus Diaries" for the *New Haven Independent*. The diaries were rich with stories of friendly drivers and portraits of bus riders from all walks of life. But the service itself was depicted as almost universally frustrating. One reporter figured out that his commute to school would take 3 hours, three buses, and a train.[1] Another got lost in the suburbs, walking through lawns and leaves on the side of the road trying to find the bus stop.[2] Many routes stopped running after 7:30, making it impossible for riders to use them to get to night class.[3]

It's true on TV. In *Insecure*, Issa crashes her car; her boarding the bus the next day is a sign of how precarious her life has become.[4] In *Broad City*, Abbi has to retrieve a package from a distant island; her stepping on a bus is a sight gag, a sign that she is going to a truly obscure part of the city.[5] In the premiere episode of *Atlanta*, Donald Glover's character Earn boards a MARTA bus with his baby daughter, feeling like he isn't going anywhere in life. He spills to a fellow rider: "I just keep losing. I mean, are some people just supposed to lose?"[6]

It's true even in America's biggest cities, with the most extensive public transportation systems. In 2017, the New York City transit organizing group Riders Alliance asked its members to submit anecdotes about their experiences on the city's above-ground transit network. They were published in a brochure that I find heartbreaking to read, a stress-inducing litany of missed doctor's appointments and blown job interviews. A home health aide was an hour late for her shift, so her co-worker had to wait an extra hour to be relieved. A Queens man was so late to a concert that he missed the entire show. A woman who worked at the mall was on her "final warning, about to get fired." The pamphlet was titled *Woes on the Bus: Frustration and Suffering, All Through the Town.*

Americans take 4.7 billion trips a year on publicly run buses. Yet most decisionmakers barely give the bus a second thought. Across the United States, the public agencies that deliver bus service are run by board members who never use it. Some of the country's largest cities don't employ anyone dedicated to improving trips for bus riders. Business leagues, community foundations, and civic leaders are often preoccupied with streetcars, hyperloops, driverless vehicles, and other projects they view as more innovative, prestigious, or likely to drive development.

Others actively try to stop bus improvements, such as business owners who fight bus shelters that they claim attract "the wrong element," legislators who ban bus-only lanes on state roads, and congressmembers who try to cut federal transit funding every year.

This combination of indifference and hostility leads to a neglect that makes so many of the bus trips we take miserable: plodding, unpredictable, uncomfortable, and circuitous. Bus speeds have fallen as city traffic gets worse; bus routes that haven't changed in decades have become less relevant as job centers change; new transportation modes provide alternatives for those who might otherwise take the bus. In many cities, the bus system has stood still, even as streets, neighborhoods, and the marketplace have been transformed. No wonder, then, that U.S. bus ridership has experienced a lost decade, falling by 17 percent between 2008 and 2018.[7]

It doesn't have to be this way. In defiance of the national trend, bus ridership has grown in cities as different as Houston, Columbus, San Francisco, Seattle, and Indianapolis. Although these places are different from one another, they share a key similarity: Their leaders have taken forceful action to improve bus service. In these and in many other cities around the country, a rising generation of activists, planners, and elected leaders have recognized the power of better bus service to offer affordable mobility and connect citizens with jobs, schools, healthcare, and everything they need to live their lives.

We need to understand, replicate, and build on their successes, because better bus service and better public transit are essential to making cities work. When we turn around the bus, we make our cities better places to live and help address some of America's deepest problems.

Public Transit Makes Cities Work

The typical private car carries between one and two people in a box that takes up over 100 cubic feet. As far as space is concerned, this is one of the least efficient ways to move people that has ever been conceived.

The National Association of City Transportation Officials (NACTO) lays the math out simply in its *Transit Street Design Guide*. Add bus service to a road and you can easily double the number of people it carries—even more so if buses are given dedicated space on the street or if a train runs down it. When you see a photograph of a bus in city traffic, there's a decent chance that the bus is carrying more people than all the cars in the frame.

Cars also eat away at cities because they need to be stored. In cities such as Hartford, Connecticut, where the amount of off-street

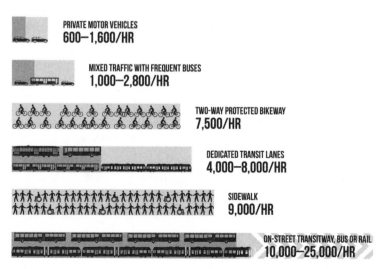

PRIVATE MOTOR VEHICLES
600–1,600/HR

MIXED TRAFFIC WITH FREQUENT BUSES
1,000–2,800/HR

TWO-WAY PROTECTED BIKEWAY
7,500/HR

DEDICATED TRANSIT LANES
4,000–8,000/HR

SIDEWALK
9,000/HR

ON-STREET TRANSITWAY, BUS OR RAIL
10,000–25,000/HR

Figure 0.1   Transit has the ability to carry substantially more people than private vehicles. (Image courtesy National Association of City Transportation Officials.)

parking tripled between 1960 and 2000 to accommodate drivers, neighborhoods can look like desolate, unattractive moonscapes. The parking lots also bring in less tax revenue than productive uses such as offices and stores.[8] To paraphrase a slogan from the Institute for Transportation and Development Policy, "more parking" means "less city" for everyone to enjoy.

When we turn around the bus, we make our cities better places to live and help address some of America's deepest problems.

Transit reduces this need, another reason it is the most efficient way to move people who are traveling to similar destinations. This makes it essential infrastructure for cities, allowing for the compactness that makes urban economies work and helps city neighborhoods thrive. That's why cities in most developed countries feature extensive urban transit networks, with rail lines in the densest corridors and convenient bus service in between.

But U.S. cities have an aversion to transit, rooted in American history and politics, that is leading us toward disaster.

The Unequal, Polluting Transportation Status Quo

In the decades after World War II, American metropolitan areas sprawled outward, fueled by the massive Interstate Highway System, which made distant suburbs possible, and by mortgage financing through agencies such as the Federal Housing Administration, which gave white Americans (almost exclusively) the means to move to the suburbs.

It's well documented that these programs intentionally furthered segregation. Richard Rothstein's *The Color of Law* offers a concise history of state and federal highway departments purposefully choosing to build roads through African American neighborhoods, often using coded language to make the case. The American Road Builders Association wrote that building interstate highways "could contribute in a substantial manner to the elimination of slum and deteriorated areas." States bulldozed black districts across the country, including in Detroit; Miami; Los Angeles; and Camden, New Jersey. Referring to the latter case, the

New Jersey attorney general's office determined that "it is obvious from a glance . . . that an attempt is being made to eliminate the Negro and Puerto Rican ghetto areas by . . . building highways that benefit white suburbanites, facilitating their movement from the suburbs to work and back."[9]

Compared with the rest of the developed world, the United States also starved public transit. Although the federal government has supported construction of new rail systems, these lack the supportive networks of frequent bus service that exist in countries such as Canada and Australia.

Starting in the 1950s, several regions rebelled against this trend. Citizens in Portland and New York defeated highway proposals; leaders in Washington, DC and Seattle agreed to invest in transit, and their regions grew in more compact ways.

But overall, the United States has continued to sprawl, and most regions have replicated this style of development.[10] Highway infrastructure and enormous parking lots built to serve highway commuters blight central neighborhoods in many cities. Between 1980 and 2014, the U.S. population grew by 41 percent, but urban road mileage grew by 77 percent.[11]

And federal and state transportation policy continue to starve urban transit. Highways get roughly four of every five federal transportation dollars. States have broad authority and large budgets to widen roads, while cities that hope to improve transit typically must navigate competitive, multistep federal grant programs, convince citizens to vote to raise local taxes, or both.

Our transportation status quo has worsened social mobility. A long commute is one of the biggest barriers to escaping poverty, according to Harvard's Equality of Opportunity project, and upward mobility is far lower in sprawling regions.[12] In car-dependent cities, paying thousands of dollars a year to fuel and maintain a private vehicle is the price of entry to the library, the market that sells fresh vegetables, or the church that speaks to our soul.

For those who don't or can't make that choice, the result is a smaller life. One study of low-wage workers in San Diego found that those who drove could access *thirty* times as many potential jobs as those who did not.[13] Youth without access to a car are less likely to work and participate in after-school activities.[14]

Nondrivers are even shut out of the democratic process. On an episode of public radio program *On the Media*, Kafui Attoh, a professor of urban studies at the City University of New York School of Labor and Urban Studies, described a conversation he overheard between two women riding the bus in Poughkeepsie, New York, which was debating plans to consolidate its bus system with a separate system run by county government:

> These are people who rely on the bus every day and they're talking about, they're like "What is consolidation going to mean for me?" The bus driver . . . he's like, "Look, you guys have great comments; the debates are happening right now at City Council meetings, and you should go." And one or two of the people were like, "Yeah, but the buses stop running at 6:30, and the City Council meeting starts after the buses stop running, so there's no way I would be able to get home." You know, even having a conversation on the future of buses was limited by the bus system itself.[15]

Given these circumstances, even many low-income families seek to buy cars. Doing so unlocks opportunities but creates new sources of precarity: broken transmissions, impound fees, even jail time due to unpaid tickets. Poor families tend to go in and out of car ownership, buying a vehicle when they can afford it and relinquishing it after an unexpected expense.[16] In 2018, more Americans held automobile debt than at any other point in history; automobile debt increased by 75 percent from 2009 to 2018, standing at $1.26 trillion.[17]

An unintended consequence of this exclusionary transportation policy is that our mobility infrastructure threatens the planet itself. Over the last 30 years, the United States has made remarkable progress in cleaning up the power sector, driving greenhouse gas emissions below 1990 levels. But the opposite is true when it comes to transportation, which is now the largest contributor to U.S. greenhouse gas emissions.[18] International Energy Agency statistics show that America has paved and sprawled its way to the most energy-intensive transportation system in the developed world.[19] It is also one of the only developed countries where the energy intensity of transportation continues to get worse. And as one of the largest emitters, the United States must make some of the largest contributions toward reducing emissions if we are to limit global warming.

Public transit can help. It causes some people to switch to transit for trips they would have otherwise driven. It makes it possible for cities to develop more densely, which means residents and visitors make fewer long driving trips and more transit, walking, biking, and short drives. A viable transit system makes it politically possible to increase the cost of driving through congestion or parking by reducing the impacts on everyone, especially low-income people.

Nondrivers are even shut out of the democratic process.

I care about transit because I want every person to have the opportunity to live a good life and because I hope to have a planet worth living on. Sprawl is killing us; cities and regions oriented around great transit are part of the way back.

There Is No Deus ex Tesla

What about Uber, or hyperloop, or driverless cars? Today, city leaders are often told that new transportation technologies will make transit obsolete. But none of the technologies that promise to transform transportation outperform transit's greatest strength: capacity.

In 2018, Elon Musk's Boring Company was awarded the rights to build an underground express between Chicago's Loop and O'Hare Airport. Musk claimed he would create an "electric skate" system that would carry private cars and small pods carrying up to sixteen people each.

The actual carrying capacity of this hypothetical system? About 2,000 passengers an hour.[20] In other words, the electric skate will carry far fewer people than the Chicago Transit Authority's Blue Line subway, which already goes to O'Hare.

It's a similar story with Uber, Lyft, and the rest of the app-enabled ride companies (known as transportation network companies [TNCs]). They have exploded in popularity. In 2012 (the year Lyft debuted and the year after Uber launched in New York City) Americans took 1.4 billion trips in for-hire vehicles, mostly taxis. By 2017, this had grown to 3.3 billion, mostly in Ubers and Lyfts.[21]

But (if you'll recall the NACTO diagram from earlier) a single lane of a city street can carry perhaps 1,600 people an hour in cars; no advanced routing algorithm can magically fit more people into Chicago's State Street or Los Angeles' Hollywood Boulevard. Only the spatial magic of public transportation can accomplish that.

These technologies also have yet to prove they can offer affordable mobility. Most of Uber and Lyft's customers are wealthy. TNC users in households that make more than $200,000 a year take more than forty-five TNC trips a year. Customers in households that make less than $15,000 take just six. Even so, Uber posts large losses every quarter; its rides are subsidized with billions of dollars in venture capital, even though its drivers are low-wage independent contractors.[22]

What so many private sector transportation innovators offer is not scalable mass mobility but boutique express service. Not surprisingly, Elon Musk envisions charging $25 to ride his Chicago electric skate.

When it comes to decarbonizing transportation, we also need to look past technological magic bullets. Electric vehicles are a hugely needed solution, but climate scientists have repeatedly found that they are not sufficient on their own. California's Air Resources Board found that even if every car in the state were electric, and 75 percent of the electricity came from renewable sources, driving would need to decline by 15 percent for the state to reach its climate goals.[23] In Hawaii, a 100 percent electric vehicle policy will not be enough to end the state's dependence on imported oil without complementary policies, including transit, that can convince people to drive less.[24] Project Drawdown, one of the most comprehensive efforts to model the ability of different policies to reduce greenhouse gases, has concluded that the most immediate transportation priority in urban areas is not electric vehicle policy but maximizing the share of trips taken by bicycle and public transit.[25]

What so many private sector transportation innovators offer is not scalable mass mobility but boutique express service.

Government leaders can't make a passive bet that the market will absolve them of responsibility. Over the last half-century, relying on the private sector to fill the gap has mostly resulted in an expensive dependence on the automobile. More recently, it has led to on-demand services that offer convenience for many trips but cannot scale for the masses. High-quality train and bus service is the mature, proven technology that American cities must deploy broadly, today, to make transportation more efficient, sustainable, and inclusive.

Fighting for Bus Service That People Can Build Their Lives Around

The bus demands particular attention for two reasons. One, buses can be improved quickly. Two, there's an enormous mismatch between how badly American cities need good bus service and how committed their leaders are to providing it. Every major city in America has streets where, if the bus were made more convenient, transit agencies would reap a bumper crop of new riders. In doing so, cities would instantly take a step toward becoming more inclusive and sustainable.

Journalists, pundits, and analysts have repeatedly discovered that the bus is a solution to urban transportation problems that is hiding in plain sight. In 2013, *Slate*'s Matthew Yglesias implored cities to "get on the bus."[26] In 2017, CNN reported that "cities realize they must fix the sorry state of buses."[27] The following year, Laura Bliss launched an entire series in *CityLab* on buses with the motto, "Love the Bus, Save Your City."[28]

It seems simple, almost embarrassingly so. And yet, the fact that the same article keeps being written shows that it is anything but simple. For more than a decade, I've worked with mayors, legislators, planners, business leaders, advocates, philanthropists, and many others working to improve the bus. I talked to dozens more while writing this book. What I've learned over those years and those conversations is that although the bus is fundamental to making transit useful, it is also fundamentally misunderstood.

Because so few decisionmakers ride buses in America, many conceive of buses and the people who ride them in ways that rely on old stereotypes and outdated planning ideas. They may think that bus riders are simply poor people with no alternatives and that it's impossible to entice people onto the bus. Or they might imagine that, because the bus carries a stigma, the most important strategy to get people to ride is to "make the bus sexy" through technological features such as USB chargers and free Wi-Fi. They might think of transit primarily as a tool to get people to work, sending buses to distant suburbs as new employers open.

The reality is more prosaic. More people choose buses when they are a useful option for them—when it's reasonably fast, affordable, and convenient. Decades of research by academics and public agencies show that this is determined mostly by factors such as how often the bus runs, how fast it is compared with alternatives, how reliable it is, and how safe riders feel.

Planners also know that how we build cities affects how convenient buses are. When neighborhoods are reasonably compact, with many destinations within a comfortable walk, bus service becomes more efficient and attractive. And they know that commutes are only a small fraction of the trips people make. City leaders must understand these principles so they can plan bus systems that that offer frequent, fast, reliable service both to jobs and to grocery stores, schools, recreation, and other destinations.

But they'll have to work for it. In every American city where I've seen buses improve, it has happened only through reformers inside and outside of government working in concert.

In an ideal world, responsive politicians and empowered public servants would simply recognize that cities need more and better transit, and they would deliver it. In the cities we actually live in, broken politics and planning practices repeatedly deliver the wrong results. Making buses a better option requires tough decisions, such as redesigning routes, removing stops, and taking space away from automobiles.

But formal public engagement and input processes tend to privilege more organized and wealthier residents, and informal networks of power reinforce that tendency. In many cities, buses and the people who ride them have been ignored for so long that it takes a fight just to get on the public agenda. For these reasons, it's often civic activists who get the conversation started: grassroots volunteers, community organizations, progressive philanthropists, or even business groups who see the link between better buses and bigger labor pools.

Often, it takes only a handful of energetic and smart collaborators to start changing the trajectory of transit in a city. In Miami, two energetic advocates almost single-handedly initiated the conversation about bus service. In Houston, one transit advocate impressed an incoming mayor enough that he was named to the board of directors of the transit agency; he became the driving force behind a bus network redesign.

But it takes a broader movement to see change through. Rapid, sustained transportation change rarely happens without an alliance between creative, fearless, independent advocates; politicians willing to stand up for transit; and visionary bureaucrats who can communicate transit's value in ways that inspire members of the public and potential political allies.

In every American city where I've seen buses improve, it has happened only through reformers inside and outside of government working in concert.

The need for strong public agency leaders is often overlooked, but it's essential to actually deliver the bus service we need. In places where transit has improved, it's often because public agency leaders were nimble, strategic, and willing to discard the by-the-book practices and processes that hamstring change efforts. Agencies have to do better than "open houses" that draw eight people at the library and instead think seriously about how to get public input that equitably represents bus riders and activates allies throughout the planning process. They have to discard ponderous project development processes that result in 5-year timelines for bus lane projects and try tactical approaches that change streets overnight instead.

Consistently delivering better bus service requires public agencies to grow stronger over time, with enough planners to maintain a constant pipeline of transit improvement projects, enough dispatchers to keep buses on time, and enough communications and outreach staff to bring transit riders' and stakeholders' voices into the conversation.

Why do I say reformers need to "win the fight" instead of using a phrase that sounds more collaborative, like "build the case for better buses," or "make friends and influence people so they love the bus"?

It's not because transit advocacy is inherently antagonistic. But reformers can't fool themselves into thinking that they can win better bus service solely through creative data, sound technical analysis, or careful messaging. The route to better buses winds through hostile ground: business owners who don't want to lose parking, suburban mayors who refuse to pay for downtown bus service, and state and federal lawmakers who want to kill government funding for transit entirely. Some of these actors can be persuaded or bargained with. More often, transit reformers have to outmaneuver, out-organize, and outvote them.

Building public understanding of transit, political coalitions committed to improving it, and transportation agencies that can effectively deliver it are challenging tasks. When you look at what transit reformers have accomplished, it often looks like a series of incremental victories: a bus network redesign one year, a more logical fare policy the next, a set of rapid bus projects the next.

The car dependency of our cities was built over decades, and undoing it means fixing many systems. Better bus service ultimately demands changing how we design our streets, run our bureaucracies, prioritize our budgets, and plan our cities. This may seem like an enormous mountain to climb. The good news is that each step toward better buses makes thousands of people's lives better.

Better Buses, Better Cities

We hear a lot of difficult stories about the bus. But after more than a decade working in transportation, I've heard plenty of hopeful ones, and I'll share them with you in the hopes of inspiring and informing your own fight for better buses.

This book is half technical backgrounder, half political field manual. If you're an activist or politician, you'll be a better one by understanding the planning principles of useful transit. If you're a transportation planner, your plans will go further with an understanding of how to get the public on your side.

I begin with an explanation of what bus riders want and how to plan bus networks that are useful to as many people as possible. After that, a series of chapters explain different elements of good bus service (such as frequency, reliability, and walkability) and how reformers have fought to achieve them. I also discuss broader issues, such as the role of new mobility modes, how state and federal politics affect bus service in American cities, and the need for a stronger transit reform movement in America.

The good news is that each step toward better buses makes thousands of people's lives better.

A nation where we realized the potential of urban buses would be a safer one. It would be a fairer one, where working-class people had more affordable, reliable ways to get to work, school, and everything that cities have to offer. It would be a more inclusive one, with more access for young people, people with disabilities, and those who don't drive. It would be a healthier, more sustainable one.

From what I've seen, I am convinced that cities have the ability to unleash the bus from unclear goals, congested streets, austerity politics, and low expectations. When politicians, activists, and public agency leaders work in concert, they can make the bus a great way to get around every American city.

Here's how to do it in yours.

01   WHAT MAKES PEOPLE CHOOSE THE BUS?

—

One of the most corrosive ideas in the transportation world, one that shows up in both the technical literature and politicians' attitudes, is the belief that most people who ride the bus have no alternative, and they'll keep riding regardless of how bad the service gets.

To use the technical jargon, the idea I'm referring to is that there are two types of transit customer. Some academic and agency studies define some people as "choice riders," who own cars but choose to ride transit because it's fast or affordable or pleasant. "Captive riders," on the other hand, don't have a car and therefore (according to the definition) are "captive" to transit.

Perhaps you can hear the disdain in the term *captive rider*. If not, you can certainly hear it in the way the concept is understood by politicians, pundits, and even some transit executives. Writing in the economics blog Freakonomics in 2009, Clemson University associate professor Eric Morris declared, "There are two major constituencies for mass transit . . . wealthier workers who commute to jobs in city centers where parking is expensive . . . [and] the very poor." The head of the Chicago Transit Authority (CTA), Dorval Carter, even told a reporter, "The people who have to ride CTA will ride CTA. The choice riders are the ones you really covet."[1]

This kind of thinking often results in a two-tiered approach to transit planning: high-end, expensive transit built to the suburbs to "entice people out of their cars" (because it's hard to bag those finicky "choice riders") and terrible bus service for everyone else.

One big problem with this idea is that it isn't true. A great many people without a car have options for getting around besides the local bus. They might use private or informal transit, such as the fleets of jitney minibuses that commuters use to get around northern New Jersey, or the unlicensed taxis that exist in many cities. They might arrange a carpool or a ride from a friend. They might ride a bike for miles, or even walk for 10 miles to their job.

The captive–choice binary doesn't have its roots in a deep sociological study of how people make transportation decisions. Like so much else that has proven harmful in the transportation industry, it comes from reductive computer models. Two Canadian transit researchers, David Crowley and Brendon Hemily, trace the concept of choice and captive riders back to the early 1960s.[2]

When researchers have looked into how "captive" non–car owners really are to transit, they repeatedly find that people do not fit into a neat binary. In 2016, my colleagues at TransitCenter and I surveyed 3,000 people in seventeen U.S. regions about their travel behavior. The resulting report, *Who's On Board*, found that people who lived near better transit took it more often, regardless of whether they owned a car. A 2003 Transportation Research Board paper found that transportation models often underestimate the mode choices available to transit riders without cars.[3] A Mineta Transportation Institute study of bus riders in Broward County, Florida, found that "rather than being a fixed amount regardless of service quality," transit ridership by people who do not own cars "increases tremendously" if transit becomes faster.[4]

Kurt Luhrsen, vice president of service planning at METRO, the transit agency in Houston, said, "You can provide such horrible bus service that even the poorest of the poor, who have no car, will find a way to get around, whether it be friends, a bike, walking, it will happen. You provide a good service, you'll have customers. You don't, you won't."

People who don't ride transit often assume that no one but poor people will ride a bus. They may believe that people choose transportation modes because they are cool or flashy. In the words of a writer for an Austin alt-weekly, "Everyone knows it, so let's say it: Buses lack sex appeal and yuppie appeal."[5]

Mary Skelton Roberts, co-director of the climate program at the Barr Foundation, said the conflation of buses with poverty "is an American construct—building buses that are low quality in neighborhoods that are already struggling. That does not have to be the reality."

It isn't the reality in places that have good bus service, as professors Ralph Buehler (of Virginia Tech) and John Pucher (of Rutgers) found when they compared the 2009 nationwide travel surveys conducted in the United States and Germany.[6] The typical American bus rider had a household income under $25,000 a year, less than half what the average U.S. household made. In Germany, the average bus rider belonged to a household that made more than $50,000 a year—no different from the typical German family.

We can see the difference in American cities, too. The median income of Los Angeles Metro bus riders is just $16,200; 61 percent live below the poverty line.[7] But does this mean that bus service is "for" poor people? As UCLA professor Michael Manville points out, only 6 percent of poor workers in the Los Angeles region use transit as their primary commute mode. Transit in the L.A. region is used primarily by low-income people, but it doesn't serve them well, and so most low-income people have chosen other ways to get around.

Meanwhile, a third of bus riders in King County, Washington (which includes Seattle) have household annual incomes above $100,000; 27 percent of New York City bus riders make more than $75,000.[8]

Everyone chooses transit more often when it meets their needs. What are those?

What Bus Riders Want

Transit service that is useful to most people satisfies seven basic criteria:

- The service goes where you want to go.
- The service runs frequently enough that you don't have to think about it.
- The service is reasonably fast.
- The service is reliable (you don't have to worry about major delays).
- You can conveniently walk from the service to your final destination.
- The service is comfortable and feels safe.
- The service is affordable.

Survey after survey has confirmed the importance of these factors (which are discussed in the following chapters).

When you recognize these criteria, you can understand why attractive, amenity-laden, flashy transit projects fail. Atlanta's streetcar, for example, fails because it gets caught in traffic, and it doesn't connect to enough destinations. The Northstar rail line in the Twin Cities basically runs through open fields to sparsely populated suburbs; there simply isn't enough around to generate ridership.

You also see that there's little use in planning transit based on its technology. Bus and rail lines across the country attract riders under the same circumstances: when they are fast, frequent, and connect many destinations that can be walked to.

David Bragdon, the executive director of TransitCenter, has said that arguing about whether trains are better than buses is like arguing about whether jackets are better than sweaters. You need both to have a full wardrobe, and you should wear whichever is appropriate for the situation you find yourself in. That means when you need to carry many thousands of people an hour, or move them quickly over long distances, you probably need a train. When you want to carry a few thousand people an hour, buses can get the job done if they are designed to be fast and reliable.

Bus and rail lines across the country attract riders under the same circumstances: when they are fast, frequent, and connect many destinations that can be walked to.

We can also dismiss the idea that we "need to make the bus sexy." In March 2016, New York Governor Andrew Cuomo announced the purchase of new buses that had a bold paint scheme, Wi-Fi, and dozens of charging ports for phones and other devices. "It has that European flair to it," he said of a bus rendering. "It has almost a Ferrari-like look."[9]

But New York City's buses are among the slowest in the country. A vehicle that looks "Ferrari-like" but moves at an average speed of 8 miles per hour is not very attractive, one reason why the city has lost bus ridership for several years in a row.

Instead, we need to plan transit networks that maximize opportunity, that let you choose from many jobs, shop at many places, visit many friends and family members. Planners can do this by providing frequent, fast, walkable bus service to as many destinations as possible.

There Are Many Trips for the Bus to Compete For

Note that I didn't say that cities should build bus networks that maximize access to jobs. I said they should maximize access to destinations. That's because more than two-thirds of transit trips (and four-fifths of all trips) are noncommute trips.[10]

For this reason, there are usually more people who use the bus in a city than decisionmakers realize. We tend to talk about "drivers," "cyclists," and "transit riders" as if people only drive, bike, or take transit.

This might be because the U.S. Census and American Community Survey "journey to work" data, which are some of the most ubiquitously cited in transportation discussions, measure only the respondent's primary commuting mode. A woman who drives 3 days a week to a part-time job and takes the bus to a different part-time job is not counted as a transit rider by the census. Neither is someone who takes the bus to college during the week and drives to a weekend job.

This makes transit's constituency look pretty small. In metro Miami, for example, only 4 percent of commuters use primarily transit to get to work. In the Twin Cities region, just 5 percent do. Even in metro Boston, it's just 12 percent. But when you look at surveys that capture the diversity of how people actually get around, you get a bigger picture. According to the census's 2013 American Housing Survey, one in five Miami households include someone who uses transit occasionally. In the Twin Cities, one in four do. And in metro Boston, 56 percent of households have a transit rider.[11]

Most transit systems have a large pool of customers who have experienced transit but have not committed to frequent use. Researchers from UCLA, examining recent transit ridership declines in Los Angeles, have concluded that most of the ridership loss was coming from a few formerly heavy transit users who had left the system. LA Metro could make up the gap just by convincing occasional transit riders to use the system a few more times a week.[12] This means planners should not overfocus service on peak commute times at the expense of midday and weekend service.

Because bus service is so deeply misunderstood by many decisionmakers, simply explaining what makes people choose transit can be enough to start changing places for the better.

Miami's Transit Alliance Rewrites the Story

In 2017, transit ridership in Miami-Dade County, Florida was in freefall. The county's politicians spent plenty of time talking about transit—but nearly all of it took the form of disputes over where to build the next big transit line in the region and what mode it should be. County mayor Carlos Gimenez sought to cancel plans to build rail, suggesting the county should investigate a Chinese-made "trackless train" (a semiautomated bus) instead.[13]

In the meantime, the local bus system, which carried two-thirds of riders, had been steadily eroding. Buses took circuitous routes, were often late, and even suffered from basic reliability issues such as broken fareboxes and hurricane-damaged bus shelters that were not fixed for months. Between 2014 and 2017, bus ridership fell from 77 million boardings to 58 million. Between March 2017 and March 2018, the county made three sets of bus service cuts affecting 38 routes, and the media largely echoed the framing that cuts were needed to achieve budget savings.[14]

This started to change with the emergence of an independent civic organization, the Transit Alliance. Founded by a Miami native, Marta Viciedo, and Azhar Chougle, who came to Miami from New York, the Alliance reset the debate in a matter of months. (Before founding Transit Alliance, Viciedo had started a political action committee that would endorse politicians who supported sustainable transportation policy. But she couldn't find enough candidates worth endorsing.)

In May 2018, the organization launched the "Where's My Bus?" project, a data visualization project that over the course of 5 weeks illustrated problems with the system's reliability, route design, and frequency and the fragmented jurisdiction of transit agencies.[15] The findings of that project began to repeatedly show up in articles written by the *Miami Herald* and other media outlets.

That fall, the Alliance issued report cards grading the county on its different transportation services.[16] Metrobus got a D, and Transit Alliance won still more media attention.

Simply explaining what makes people choose transit can be enough to start changing places for the better.

From there, it was off to the races—to a 24-hour bus marathon, to be exact. In December 2018, Transit Alliance members rode the system for a day straight (two Miami-Dade county commissioners and a Miami city commissioner joined them for part of the ride), an exercise that quickly revealed the fragility of the network.

Transit Alliance's stunts added up to a county-wide education on transit that grabbed the attention of decisionmakers. After Chougle and Viciedo briefed county commissioners on the "Where's My Bus?" project, they began to have more in-depth conversations with Mayor Gimenez.

They asked for—and the county gave them—a $250,000 grant to manage a redesign of Miami-Dade's flawed and neglected bus network. They matched it with another $250,000 they fundraised themselves, and the project kicked off in May 2019, aiming to transform the system over a 2-year period.

A Bus Network Worth Riding

Many cities are like Miami, where decisionmakers treated the bus and the people who rode it as an afterthought, focusing their transportation efforts on higher-profile projects. But this low-energy equilibrium can be quickly disrupted by a high-energy group, such as Transit Alliance, that offers a clear diagnosis of the challenges facing transit in a region and clear solutions.

Organizer Ai-jen Poo wrote that civic groups have many different types of potential power. Some have political power, others economic power, and others the power to disrupt government functions. Transit Alliance, at least at first, didn't seem to have any of these. They were a small group with just a few volunteers, working completely unpaid for 6 months.

And yet they wielded, in abundance, what Poo calls "narrative power": the ability to break the patterns of wrongheaded thinking that had convinced county decisionmakers that where new transit lines went, and what technology they used, were Miami's most pressing transit challenges.

"Everything around the bus system was broken, right?" Chougle said. "The way our elected officials thought and acted on it; the way our transit department did things with the bus system and the way that the media at large perceived what was going on."

Even with a small staff, Transit Alliance was able to use data, graphic design, and storytelling to craft a larger explanation of the region's transportation failure, one that reset journalists' understanding of transit and finally forced a response from politicians.

"'Where's my Bus?' validated a lot of things that people have been experiencing for a very long time," Chougle said. "It puts it in numbers and a format where anyone can sort of understand that these are real issues, and this is what's contributing to ridership decline."

Reimagining the bus network, as Transit Alliance has been tasked to do, can be one of the most important ways to start reversing that decline. To understand why, it's worth learning from some of the places that have done it.

02 MAKE THE BUS FREQUENT

—

Jarrett Walker, a transit consultant who has worked around the world, likes to say that "frequency is freedom." The difference between a bus that runs every half hour and a bus that runs every 15 minutes is the difference between planning your life around a schedule and the freedom to show up and leave when you want.

In the 2016 *Who's On Board* survey I worked on with colleagues at TransitCenter. We asked 3,000 U.S. transit riders to imagine a bus route that was infrequent, slow, crowded, and unpleasant in other ways.[1] We also asked them to rate different improvements an agency could make to the route; overwhelmingly, respondents said that the fix they wanted the most was for the agency to run the bus every 10 minutes. We found similar results in a 2019 survey.

It's especially important for short bus trips. A Los Angeles Metro study of its bus network has found that frequency has the biggest impact on trips under two-and-a-half miles, where people may spend as much time walking to and waiting at the bus stop as they do on the bus itself.[2]

From a rider's perspective, the more frequent the service, the better. Every 15 minutes is good; every 10 is better; every 8 or 5 is fantastic. On some high-capacity "bus rapid transit" systems around the world, buses may come every 2 or 3 minutes.

From a transit agency's perspective, of course, frequent service has to be justified by demand. Across the United States, transit agencies generally define "frequent service" as service that arrives at least every 15 minutes for most of the day, a good standard for local bus service but one that should be considered a floor—the bare minimum for a route to be branded as frequent.

Most cities have plenty of corridors that can justify frequent bus service. And without fail, those are the most popular routes in a city. In the Columbus, Ohio transit system, four of its sixty-eight bus routes carried 40 percent of its ridership.

The Ridership–Coverage Tradeoff

Walker argues that in any bus network, routes reflect two compet-
ing purposes[3]:

- *Ridership* routes attract riders because they are frequent, and
  they connect busy destinations quickly. This service is convenient to use and goes where lots of people want to go.
- *Coverage* routes cover geographic areas with little demand.
  These are typically infrequent, and they sometimes meander
  in order to increase the amount of area they cover. This service is inconvenient to use, but it may provide essential lifeline
  access to people who need service, or be justified by the need
  to provide service to every municipality that pays taxes into a
  district.

A network that focuses on building ridership will concentrate
frequent service along busy corridors, capturing many trips in those
corridors. One focused on coverage will provide infrequent service
all over the region, making sure everyone gets something.

Coverage routes often include deviations, because they need to
traverse a wide area to pick up the few riders waiting for them or stop
at destinations that are not on a good frequent corridor but justify
some service (such as a clinic or community center). Routes designed
for ridership, by contrast, are usually direct, because ridership arises
from offering a direct path that's useful to lots of people. Or as one
analysis of Houston's bus network put it, "[High-ridership] routes
[are] primarily straight; [low-ridership routes] largely squiggle."[4]

Transit agencies can connect frequent routes into "frequent
grids" that ask riders to transfer. On a frequent grid, at least in theory, the connecting bus should always be arriving soon.

And a bus network of multiple connecting routes that run frequently for most of the day, 7 days a week, is a network more people
can build their lives around.

To Kurt Luhrsen, vice president of service planning at Houston's
METRO transit agency, it's simple: "You want lots of people to ride
transit, you put lots of service where you have lots of people, lots of
jobs, lots of demand, and you'll get ridership."

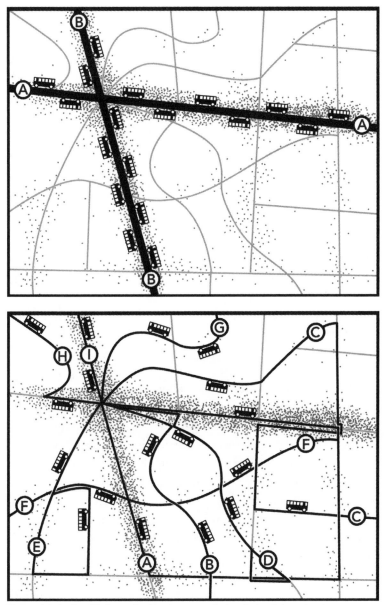

Figures 2.1a (top) and b (bottom)   Two bus networks in a fictional city, using the same
number of buses, that illustrate the ridership–coverage tradeoff. The first network focuses
service on the busiest areas; frequency and ridership are high, but some areas have no service.
The second network provides a route on every street; everyone lives near a stop, but service is
infrequent and waits are long. (Images copyright Jarrett Walker + Associates.)

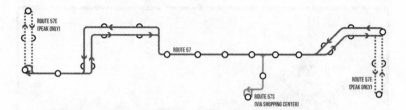

Figure 2.2   Infrequent routes often include deviations in order to cover a lot of area. (Image courtesy National Association of City Transportation Officials.)

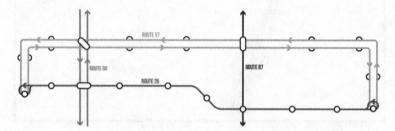

Figure 2.3   A grid of frequent bus service can rely on direct routing and transfer points to speed up buses. (Image courtesy National Association of City Transportation Officials.)

The ridership–coverage tradeoff is an elegant concept, but it's also supported by complex modeling. When researchers from the University of Utah examined data from 157 U.S. cities, they found that increasing the frequency of service on current routes was about 20 percent more effective at increasing ridership than adding more routes.[5]

When Walker works with transit agency clients, he works to make the ridership–coverage spectrum explicit. He presents it as a neutral choice, one that depends on what a community values. But many of the cities he has worked with have decided to reorient their focus on building ridership.

That's because a frequent bus network has many virtues. It serves more people while bringing down the agency's per-ride cost. It makes bus service attractive enough that more people choose it. Both of these can build political momentum for further changes.

Houston realized all those benefits after a network redesign it launched in 2015, which has become a model for agencies across the nation. Overnight, a bus system that was inflexible, narrowly focused on the city's downtown, and provided skeletal access on weekends was replaced with one that offered vastly more all-day service. A network that was shedding riders was replaced with one that opened up access to the city and recognized the power of frequent service to make the bus more useful and attractive for more people.

Understanding why Houston reimagined and reworked its bus system can teach us a lot about what makes bus service attractive—and the effort that it takes.

Houston Cleans the Slate

Houston is one of America's great and growing cities, a sprawling metropolis with more than 2.3 million residents. METRO, the transit agency serving Houston and some surrounding suburbs, had a well-regarded park-and-ride bus system; it also ran one of the highest-performing light rail lines in the country, the Red Line, which connected the city's walkable downtown, the Texas Medical Center, and adjacent neighborhoods. But local bus service was a relic.

A bus network of multiple connecting routes that run frequently for most of the day, 7 days a week, is a network more people can build their lives around.

Between 2007 and 2011, ridership had fallen by almost 20 percent. Local bus ridership was less productive (in terms of boardings per hour) than in San Antonio, Austin, and Dallas—and far below other peer agencies in Denver, Miami, and Phoenix.

Christof Spieler, an engineer and urban planner, lecturer at Rice University, and volunteer advocate with the Citizens' Transportation Coalition who often wrote about transit (and regularly used it as well), said, "It was an infrequent system. It was a system which was especially infrequent on the weekends. It was a system which was very confusing to use."

It was obvious to Spieler that the bus network had not kept up with the demographics of Houston. Most bus routes went to Houston's downtown, but they missed several other job centers that had grown over the past two decades. The system had also not responded to the suburbanization of Houston's poverty, providing little service to neighborhoods that had been middle-income in the 1980s but were now home to many low-income households.[6] This was one reason why transit ridership was falling despite the fact that the transit agency was providing more hours of service than at any point in decades.[7]

Spieler's commentary, and his growing reputation around the city, caught the eye of Houston mayor Annise Parker. Parker had been one of the few candidates to even acknowledge the role of buses during the 2009 mayoral campaign. Most of her opponents focused on light rail; Parker took a broader view.

"My answer was always 'I support light rail, but it's only a small solution in a really big city," Parker said. "I used to talk about the buses as the workhorse of the system. No one really paid any attention to that comment."

Parker chose Spieler as one of her five appointments to the nine-member METRO board. About Spieler, Parker said, "I wanted at least one transit advocate . . . someone who rode it every day, someone who was really passionate about it. It was only later that I realized that he was a transit expert."

The problems with Houston's bus network were obvious not just to Spieler but to other riders. In 2011, when METRO sought comments on its long-range plan, half of all of the feedback it received was on existing bus service.

But the agency was consumed by other issues. New board members were immediately plunged into crisis management mode after learning that METRO had violated federal procurement rules, putting planned light rail projects at risk.[8] An opportunity did not arrive until the following year, when the poor state of bus service became a political liability.

In 2013, METRO was required to ask citizens of its member jurisdictions to vote on how it should spend its dedicated sales tax revenue. The agency collected a 1-cent sales tax in those municipalities but kept only three-quarters of the collected tax receipts. The other quarter went to a "general mobility" fund, which local governments used for sidewalks, road maintenance, and other transportation projects.

Should METRO continue to give some of its tax revenue to local governments to pay for a grab bag of "general mobility" projects? Pro-transit advocates, from groups such as Houston Tomorrow and the Citizens' Transportation Coalition, said no, and one reason was because that funding could pay for additional bus service instead.[9] Transit critics were also pointing to falling bus ridership, putting additional pressure on the agency to act.

By this point, Spieler had been talking about the need to redesign the bus network for years and was one of the few agency representatives with a comprehensive response to the criticism. With Spieler dissenting, the board voted to support continuing the "general mobility" fund but responded to the criticism by putting Spieler in charge of a new strategic planning committee focused on redesigning the bus network.[10]

The committee started looking for consultants with a "request for qualifications" that laid out the challenge clearly in its opening paragraph:

> Over the past decade, METRO has lost substantial local bus ridership as [new light rail lines] replaced several well-utilized bus routes, fares were increased and passenger discounts reduced, inner city neighborhoods were redeveloped, and population growth continued to occur in areas largely outside of METRO's current service footprint. During this time, many local bus routes have remained unchanged and may or may not be well suited to changing demographics and employment opportunities in the region.[11]

The document called for ambition. It told prospective respondents that the agency wanted to "design a new regional transit system from the ground up with a 'blank slate' approach." It asked them to consider that the ideal system "might bear absolutely no resemblance to the current system." It called for someone to help METRO design "a financially sustainable future transit system that will grow ridership while evolving into more than just a transportation system of last resort for those who cannot drive."

Reflecting on the language, Spieler said, "Transit consulting firms get very used to the transit industry being cautious. We needed to [send] a really clear message that we were open to something radical."

This also helped transit staff understand that it was safe to be honest. "It gave everyone the green light to say [in outside meetings], 'we're going to start this project by talking about what we're not doing well,'" Spieler said. "It's a lot more logical than if you go to the public and say, 'we have this great local bus network, and we're going to blow it all up and start over.'"

To figure out what it would look like to start over, METRO and its consultants surveyed riders and convened a 120-person stakeholder group, including transit operators, riders, elected officials, unions, businesses, and social service agencies, that was facilitated by a local firm, Traffic Engineers, Inc., and Jarrett Walker + Associates.

After a lengthy discussion about the tradeoffs between ridership and coverage, METRO's stakeholders said that the agency should be spending at least three-quarters of its resources on frequent service that would draw ridership.[12] The existing system was about 55 percent ridership routes. Ultimately, the board adopted an official statement saying that 80 percent of its bus service would be dedicated to growing ridership, which would more than double access to frequent transit service for residents, businesses, and low-income households.

The agency wanted to "design a new regional transit system from the ground up with a 'blank slate' approach."

"We spent eight months just talking about the goals and objectives for this study," Luhrsen said. "Even as a project manager who's been doing this for 20 years, I was getting antsy." But, he admitted, this led to a level of buy-in and understanding among stakeholders and the agency's board that would prove critical later on.

With the board committed to a bus "re-imagining," the project team held a week-long design charrette with agency staff to sketch out what the new system would look like. They drew three networks: a "red" frequent network, a "blue" network of routes with 30-minute headways, and "green" hourly buses.

This plan, released in May 2014, undid the old network's undue focus on downtown, creating a wider grid that sent frequent service into south and west Houston. It would replace the region's skeletal weekend service with all-day, all-week frequency. It would vastly increase access to transit, putting a million jobs and a million households within reach of frequent transit, with no increase in the operating budget.

Even so, there was real community blowback from people whose service would be disrupted. Spieler said, "We voted to approve a draft plan in principle with two state reps standing at a podium in front of us, telling us not to vote to move forward. So the politics of this were in no way simple. It took a lot of will on the part of the board."

One critical factor was the continued support of Mayor Parker.

"I wanted to show the flag," Parker told me, "I went out [to public meetings] to make sure everybody saw that I was supportive of where the board was going." She also said that she refused to allow critics to bypass the process by going directly to her, insisting that they bring complaints to the METRO staff and board.

Some complaints focused on cuts to service in areas with low demand and a proposal to replace coverage routes with "flex zones," where on-demand service would run instead of fixed-route buses. Ultimately, METRO got rid of the flex zones and increased its operating budget so it could keep traditional coverage service. With these changes, the plan was approved in February 2015.

The approval of the draft plan set off an enormous mobilization at Houston METRO. Luhrsen had asked his superiors for 18 months to implement the redesign.

He was told to do it in 6.

This was rooted in political reality. Mayor Parker was in the last year of her final term. In November, voters would pick a new mayor, with the power to replace most of METRO's board. That meant the new network had to be on the ground before the election, and with enough time to get citizens used to it.

The scope and the speed of the project demanded an approach that was less like the typical process for adjusting bus routes and more like the precise project management techniques that a construction firm uses to build a skyscraper. The process was run through a five-person task force, which included Luhrsen, that reported directly to executive leadership and had authority across agency departments. And it was run through the "Master Schedule," a 650-line spreadsheet that attempted to map out every task agency staff would have to perform between Day One and Launch Day to make the new network a reality.

When done at scale, the most prosaic task becomes epic. Figuring out how METRO would change service information at 10,000 bus stops, for example, required conversations with six separate departments. Transit agency staff eventually settled on an ingenious solution: They installed new signs with the new network's route and schedule information, covering each with a heavy-duty bag printed with the current route information. The day before launch, each bag could be pulled off in seconds with a hooked pole, revealing the new network information with a magician's flourish.

On Tuesdays, the implementation team got updates from section managers to plug into the master schedule. On Wednesdays, they reviewed the updates to flag issues that were at risk of falling behind schedule. On Thursdays, they met with every one of METRO's division heads.

Those Thursday meetings were the time for accountability, Luhrsen said. "If [division heads] did not address the critical areas that we had already identified, we would ask probing questions, to do a little public shaming to, you know, forcefully encourage them to get back on track." The team also used these meetings to figure out whether extra staff or money was needed to keep the project on schedule and had a direct line to a key executive if they needed either.

Launch Day—August 16, 2015—was by many measures a quiet day. This was an intentional choice. Houston METRO traditionally did service changes on Sundays, the day with the lowest ridership. It was also the week before the public schools opened.

The day before, staff had gone out and switched over every bus stop. Dozens of staff ambassadors were posted at bus stops to let people know about the changes. The agency's bus operators had attended customer service training sessions scheduled over the past month. METRO's emergency management center had been activated, with operations, social media, police, and planning personnel who could help respond to issues as they came up. And fares were free for the week, to speed up boarding and avoid penalizing riders who might have gotten on the wrong bus.

METRO also took special care to look out for customers who had trouble navigating the changes. During the first week, the agency sent minibuses trawling along segments of routes that had been discontinued. When staff found riders waiting at a discontinued stop, they'd stop to explain the changes and offer to drive them to the nearest transit center where they could complete their trip.

The agency even had a taxi company on call, which customer service supervisors could dispatch to riders who called because they were late to work or otherwise in desperate straits. Luhrsen estimated that METRO paid for about 150 taxi rides, "the best money we probably spent [in terms of] the good will that it earned, and dirt cheap to do, even if you were paying $25 or $30 for the ride."

There was plenty of confusion during those first days. METRO staff were still getting questions at the downtown transit center at 10 p.m. But the chaos subsided after a few days.

About 60 percent of the system's local bus trips now take place on its frequent network.[13] METRO won the 2016 System of the Year from the American Public Transportation Association. Houston's transit ridership increased in the year after the redesign and has outpaced that of other Texas cities. In 2018, Houston was one of just a few cities where overall transit ridership increased.

> *About 60 percent of the system's local bus trips now take place on its frequent network.*

"We all wear ten-gallon hats and ride horses and drive pickup trucks, and nobody takes transit here, or at least that's what the rest of the country seems to think," Luhrsen said. "So when we were able to buck the trend on ridership, that got a lot of people's attention."

Within 2 years of Houston's launch, over a dozen cities, including Austin, Columbus, Baltimore, and Indianapolis, had redesigned their bus networks. In 2017, *Governing* magazine called network redesigns "the hottest trend in transit."[14]

Most of the transit agencies that have done it, as in Houston, have found that the effort must be structured to succeed, in a way that draws on the intelligence of every department that's involved. The Central Ohio Transit Authority built what Josh Sikich (who managed the redesign implementation) described as a "secondary organizational infrastructure" that ignored the agency's traditional departments and instead put staff in functional "working groups" (i.e., bus stops, shelters, infrastructure; government and community relations).

"At a lot of agencies, you can have people that are there for ten years who may not really interact with other departments," Sikich said.

Many transit agencies used the momentum of the redesign to bring other improvements across the finish line. For years, Todd Hemingson of Austin's Capital Metro said, the agency had been asking the city of Austin to make traffic signal and intersection changes that would have helped buses stay on time, to no avail.[15] But with a major redesign in the works, it convinced the city to make nineteen changes.

"The way to make buses better tends to be thousands of little projects, and none of them by itself is particularly exciting to an elected official," Spieler said. "One of the reasons why I believe the 'big bang' approach is worthwhile is it plays with those dynamics by making bus route scheduling—which is the most boring and ordinary of things—a big deal. When you do the project on this kind of scale, there is no doubt it's a major project. It gets media coverage; it gets political attention; it gets commitment from leadership."

The Frayed Edges of the Network

Frequency is freedom, Walker's well-known phrase says. But doesn't this suggest that in areas that receive coverage service, transit riders are less free?

It's a tough reality. As long as transit agencies are asking for cost-neutral network redesigns, staying within the same budget, a bus redesign is not a win–win but a win–lose. In fairness, a well-done redesign is more like a win–win–win–win–lose, offering better service for most current riders (including those who currently receive coverage service) and service that is more useful for more people and therefore benefits more people in the future, even as it inevitably inconveniences some riders in the hardest-to-serve places.

Luhrsen noted that when METRO and its consultants held an internal workshop to redesign its bus network, it was easy for staff to figure out where high-frequency routes should go. They spent the most time figuring out the coverage routes, because those posed the hardest questions. "You spend 90 percent of your time dealing with those lowest performing routes, and you don't spend as much time promoting and thinking about the routes . . . that carry the bulk of your service."

There's no denying that on the edges of the network, people will have their trips disrupted. Some will not have good options. The so-called Pareto improvement—a policy change that betters some people's welfare without making a single person worse off in any way—is elusive when it comes to service planning. The most ineffective, outdated bus network still serves people who have built their routines around it, routines that may no longer be tenable after a change.

> "The way to make buses better tends to be thousands of little projects, and none of them by itself is particularly exciting to an elected official."

This is not a call to freeze bus networks in amber, a policy choice that can only result in continued decline. But when it's at all possible, network redesigns should arrive with a boost in service. Some coverage can be retained or redrawn. This can soothe the frayed edges of the network, the places where few people ride the bus but may be devastated by cuts.

Houston ultimately expanded its annual operating budget for buses by 4 percent. After Richmond's network redesign, city leaders approved an additional $800,000 in funding to restore some coverage service in low-income neighborhoods.[16] Columbus's redesign came in the context of an 11 percent increase in transit service hours, phased in over 3 years.[17] Indianapolis went through a redesign involving a substantial increase in service, after voters approved new taxes to support the system (discussed in Chapter 6).

Los Angeles Metro began assessing its bus network in 2018 but has said from the beginning that the redesign will be cost-neutral, at a time when the agency is building billions of dollars' worth of new rail construction. In a letter to the agency's board, advocates warned that this "impedes what could otherwise be a meaningful opportunity to enable greater transportation access with bus service."[18] That's exactly right.

Jarrett Walker noted that, compared with agencies in Australia and Europe, his "U.S. clients always have the poorest transit budgets, requiring the most painful trade-offs."[19] Most U.S. cities have unmet demand for bus service, places where more service would be well used. The job of a consultant such as Walker is to help agencies meet that demand while understanding the implications of the tradeoffs with a constrained budget. The job of a city's leaders is to ask whether those constraints actually make sense.

Frequent Service Opens Up Cities

For bus riders, frequent service is the base of a system that you can build your life around. The ability to "walk up and go," to make spontaneous decisions about when to leave and where to travel, is a freedom unattainable to someone who has to rely on a half-hourly bus service. That's why thinking about frequency is such an important aspect of designing transit and why it's often the best place to start for reformers working in places without a history of intelligent conversation about transit.

"U.S. clients always have the poorest transit budgets, requiring the most painful trade-offs."

"The fundamental problem [with Houston's buses] was not a money problem," Spieler said. "It was more of a focus problem. [METRO staff] were focused on light-rail expansion. They were focused on making the buses themselves better and more reliable. Nobody was focused on the fundamental structure of the bus system itself. I just looked at the problems with the system, and it felt to me like something that couldn't be easily solved one little bit at a time."

One bit at a time tends to be how bus routes change when decisionmakers aren't focused on the big picture. Instead, planners make tweak after tweak in response to new developments or customer complaints. As Luhrsen explained, the reasoning is often, "We don't have money for a new route, so you split an existing route. [The result is] worse service, but there is some more coverage there."

Without someone keeping an eye on larger goals, transit agencies are often pressured to make changes rooted in parochial demands. Talking about life before the system reimagining, Luhrsen said, "On many occasions people had come before the board and berated staff about . . . a route not serving exactly what they wanted, and the board shook its finger and said, 'make this better for this person.' You make those changes year after year after year . . . [but] somebody from the outside who's considering taking transit looks at [the map] and says, 'what is this?'"

In many cities, the process of going through a bus network redesign often helps decisionmakers think about the goals of transit for the first time and draws attention to systems that may have not received much attention for many years. The decision by transit agencies in Austin, Columbus, Houston, and elsewhere to brand redesign efforts with names such as "Cap Remap" and "System Reimagining" gives them an internal and external stature that is both an honest reflection of the effort they require and important tactically.

Leaders in Houston, Austin, and Columbus are now trying to maintain the momentum from their redesigns and continue improving bus service. All three cities are planning or building rapid bus projects, designed to make their most popular bus routes faster and more dependable. That's because making buses better can start with redrawing a map, but it has to continue by redesigning the street.

03 MAKE THE BUS FAST AND RELIABLE

—

A swimming penguin. A sprinting rat. These are just a few of the things that can outpace buses in New York City, according to the watchdog group Straphangers Campaign and analysis by TransitCenter.[1] And we should be glad that Manhattan isn't on a volcanic fissure; as WNYC editor Kate Hinds pointed out on Twitter, Hawaiian lava has been clocked at almost twice the speed of some crosstown buses.[2]

And yet the sub-lava speeds of some buses is not even their worst quality. Instead, it's those buses' volatility. A bus commute that takes an hour is a drag, but a commute that takes 45 minutes one day and 75 minutes the next is far worse, because it wreaks havoc on your ability to plan.

In 2018, the think tank Center for an Urban Future researched how transit affected the lives of New York City's home health aides, who have some of the longest commutes of any profession in the city.[3] The unreliability of transit, especially on long bus routes, was an intense stressor. Arriving late could delay a colleague's ability to go home to her family or leave a patient without care. One aide interviewed in the report began leaving her home so early that she would sometimes arrive at her client's home 40 minutes before her shift started, time she received no compensation for.

Frequent bus service promises freedom, but when that bus service is unreliable, it's a false promise. The ubiquity of the phrase "must have access to reliable transportation" in job listings underscores what's at stake. Freeing buses from the chaos of city traffic can do a lot to remove chaos from bus riders' lives.

Free the Bus from City Traffic

On a map, a bus route looks like a simple line. But sitting in the operator's chair reveals incredible complexity. For example, over the course of 6 miles, a bus making a run on the B46 local route in Brooklyn crosses almost 70 streets and makes roughly 40 stops, all while pulling in and out of traffic.

This complexity breeds unreliability. Seventy intersections and forty stops is 110 possible points of variation—crossings where the bus might get a well-timed green light or sit at a red, stops where there might be a long line of people waiting to board, or none at all. That's not even counting the variability of traffic, which might move well on Tuesday and crawl during a Wednesday thunderstorm.

Hawaiian lava has been clocked at almost twice the speed of some crosstown buses.

Eventually and inevitably, this also leads to the dreaded "bus bunch," when two or more buses travel together in a caravan of misery. Once a bus starts running behind schedule, the problem tends to snowball and delay later buses. Customers pile up at the stops ahead, and boarding these larger-than-average crowds slows the bus down even more. Eventually, the bus behind catches up to the lead, and the two travel in a pair.

The big problem with bunching is not the bunch *per se* but the service gap that remains. A frequent bus route might promise service every 10 minutes. If reliability problems mean riders actually experience a 30-minute wait before a three-bus platoon arrives, they will recognize this as a false promise.

Transit staff do have strategies to break up a bus bunch, but most of them involve inconveniencing riders. The lead driver might be told to start skipping stops to get ahead of the trailing bus; the operator of the second bus might be told to kick her passengers off, sending them to the leading bus, and drive further up the route to fill the service gap. Or the leader and follower might play a confusing game of bus stop leapfrog.

It is best to design bus routes in ways that help avoid these problems to begin with. Industrial consultants have found that complex processes lead to product defects and manufacturing problems. Business improvement approaches such as Six Sigma and *kaizen* call for close audits of product assembly and business processes, in order to cut out unnecessary steps and iron out places where variability gets introduced into a product.

Bus routes can be subjected to something similar. Transit planners and engineers have a full toolkit of technologies, techniques, and designs they can use to streamline a bus route, detailed in manuals such as the National Association of City Transportation Officials' *Transit Street Design Guide.*

First, they can cut down on the amount of time the bus is stopped to pick up passengers. Many American buses stop every few blocks, sometimes every block, and on some rare occasions, multiple times on the same block! By eliminating certain stops and asking riders to walk a bit further, they can make the trip faster for everyone.

Even how bus stops get placed makes a difference. When buses have to pull over to the curb, they get delayed fighting back into traffic. On the other hand, bus stops can be "in-lane," with the sidewalk extended to meet the bus. This prioritizes the bus: Instead of bus riders waiting for drivers to pass, drivers wait for bus riders to board.

They can also let riders board at every door (asking them to pre-pay at a machine at the bus stop or tap their farecard on a validator on the bus). Dipping a magnetic stripe fare card takes 5 seconds per person, on average. All-door boarding reduces this to less than 2 seconds.[4] At busy bus stops, the math is formidable. In San Francisco, after all-door boarding was introduced across the system, buses spent 40 percent less time at stops.[5]

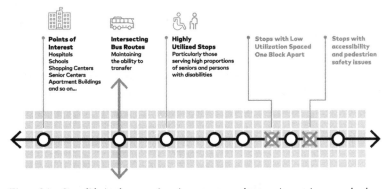

Figure 3.1   Consolidating bus stops is an important way that transit agencies can make the bus faster. (Image courtesy TransitCenter.)

Figure 3.2   In this example of a bus "queue jump," the bus pulls into a short bus-only lane on the right side of the street. It then gets a short bus-only signal, allowing it to beat other traffic across the intersection. (Image courtesy National Association of City Transportation Officials.)

Finally, they can free the bus from city traffic by giving the bus its own lane. In congested corridors, long stretches of bus lane can let riders breeze through. On other routes, a short stretch of bus lane can help the bus get through a congested spot. Or, buses can get a "queue jump" at intersections, with a short stretch of bus-only lane. The bus gets its own signal to proceed before the green light for general traffic, allowing the bus to cut to the head of the line and escape the scrum of cars in the intersection.

Of course, bus-only lanes don't make much of a difference when they're blocked by parked cars and trucks making deliveries. Painting bus lanes red has been widely shown to help with "self-enforcement." When buses get the red-carpet treatment, other vehicles are up to 50 percent less likely to block the lane.[6]

For those who insist on blocking buses anyway, the best answer is a combination of nearby commercial loading zones and automated photo enforcement, although many states still don't allow bus-lane cameras.

At intersections, cities can install transit signal priority technology, which lets traffic signal controllers and buses "talk" with each other. A bus that arrives at an intersection might get an early green light. A green light that is about to end might stay green a little longer so that bus riders can get through. In New York City, installing signal priority on bus routes has cut end-to-end run times by as much as 19 percent.[7]

"For bus systems it's really important that the DOT take the perspective that we are a partner with the transit agency," Scott Kubly, who was then the director of Seattle's Department of Transportation, said in a 2017 interview. In most cities, the municipal government controls streets and intersections, and a separate transit agency controls service levels, boarding procedures, and stop spacing. "To use an analogy, if we were running a railroad, it would be as if one department controlled the tracks and another department controlled the trains. . . . You have to act as if you are one entity pursuing the same goal, which is moving transit faster. Where we have a high volume of buses that are full of people, we're going to allocate the right-of-way for those buses to move as quickly and as reliably as possible."[8]

When cities and transit agencies do all of this, there's less that can go wrong in the complex process of a bus running its route. A crush of riders can board in a minute, not three. The bus doesn't get caught at red lights as often or have to maneuver around as many parked trucks.

Brooklyn's B46 bus, the complex route I described at the start of the chapter, has been worked over and slimmed down by New York City Transit and the city's Department of Transportation. The resulting B46 "Select Bus Service" is a typical example of how many American cities apply rapid bus treatments to individual bus routes. The Select Bus has off-board fare collection, bus lanes on part of the route, and transit signal priority. Whereas the local bus makes forty stops in fewer than 6 miles, the Select Bus stops just thirteen times. Even with imperfect enforcement of bus lanes, the difference is notable. Where the local crawls along at 5.7 mph, the Select Bus is 7.8 mph.[9] Just one in ten Select Bus Service buses is bunched, compared with one in seven of the local buses.

Several cities now have at least one rapid bus line. In the Seattle region, King Country Metro's RapidRide routes have cut travel times (up to 19 percent) and increased customer satisfaction; ridership on those lines grew by 43 percent after they got the rapid bus treatment, at a per-rider cost 21 percent *lower* than on non-RapidRide buses.[10]

Unlike increases in frequency (which cost transit agencies money), speeding up the bus saves transit agencies on their operating budget. When a route gets faster, fewer buses and drivers are needed to provide good service. An analysis of Washington, DC's transit system found that if the agency could improve bus speeds by 1 mph, the agency's costs would decrease by 4 percent.[11]

New York has always been a busy, congested place with busy, congested streets. But bus speeds have continued to get worse in recent years, falling to 7.4 mph in 2016.[12] The same story has been seen in many of America's cities. In Philadelphia, bus speeds fell every year from 2014 to 2017, and most buses travel below 12 mph.[13] Average vehicle speeds have decreased at most transit agencies since 2012, according to the National Transit Database.[14]

"For bus systems it's really important that the DOT take the perspective that we are a partner with the transit agency."

Among the culprits is the enormous increase in Uber and Lyft rides; Amazon and other retailers have also led to a doubling in urban freight traffic associated with online shopping.[15] This means even more can go wrong for buses and is going wrong for their riders. Cities have to break out the toolkit and start fixing the streets for transit.

Unbunch My Bus

Most bus routes are governed by a schedule that tells them when to leave the terminal and when to stop at specific stops. This is true even on frequent routes. A bus rider may read on the transit agency website that "service runs every 10 minutes between 7 a.m. and 7 p.m." But bus operators usually still refer to a schedule that tells them to leave the depot at 6:58, 7:08, 7:18, and so on, wait at Ashland Mall until 7:33, 7:43, 7:53, and so on, and end their run at the depot at 8:02, 8:12, 8:22, and so on.

In theory, transit agencies write bus schedules with enough slack so that on slow-running days, the bus is able to stay on time, while on fast-running days the bus operator waits at designated "control points" until it's time to leave.

Unreliability throws an enormous wrench into this process. Simon Berrebi, a postdoctoral fellow at Georgia Tech who wrote his dissertation on bus bunching, said he regularly sees bus routes that are so unreliable that they might be able to run the route in 30 minutes on a fast day but take 80 minutes on a slow one. There is no way to write a schedule that effectively splits the difference between these extremes.

"Eighty percent of the time the bus will arrive early, will just sit at the control point and waste time," Berrebi said. "But [the worst] 20 percent of buses—you know, it's raining, there's congestion, there's construction—when that happens, the schedule is completely unable to control that. So essentially, you have a schedule that wastes time when you don't need it, and is unable to control the system when you do need it."

Instead, agencies have to manage bunching as it happens, which requires hiring enough dispatchers to monitor buses in the field and staying disciplined. In the late 2000s, the Chicago Transit Authority instituted a series of management shifts to instill accountability and a sense of competition between bus managers, including a monthly "Unbunching" meeting where the heads of all eight bus garages meet to compare their performance on reducing bunching.[16]

Transit agencies can also ditch the schedule entirely, focusing on keeping buses evenly spaced instead of trying to adhere to schedules that leave bus riders waiting around on fast days and are unattainable on slow days. This "headway-based management" also requires more attention from dispatchers or high-quality real-time information on buses.

What about Bus Rapid Transit?

Many cities around the world have high-capacity systems known as bus rapid transit (BRT). These are high-end systems, often described as "light rail on rubber tires," that can carry tens of thousands of people an hour in dedicated transitways and infrastructure-intensive, metro-like stations. These types of systems are appropriate mostly in the same sorts of dense places where light rail can operate.

Many American cities, on the other hand, have watered down the term *bus rapid transit* to refer to far more modest rapid bus improvements. Partly to counter that, the Institute for Transportation and Development Policy (ITDP), a global nonprofit that helps governments implement BRT, has a 100-point scale that ranks BRT lines on everything from how much dedicated right-of-way they have, to the strength of their branding and customer information, to their integration with the rest of the transit network and bicycling.[17]

For its intended purpose, helping transit planners around the world understand the different aspects of high-capacity BRT systems, it's a useful tool. However, there is also a risk of getting too caught up in the rankings.

In Cleveland, for example, the HealthLine BRT line gets a silver ranking from ITDP and is touted on the transit agency's website as a national model. But Cleveland mayor Frank Jackson seems to hate local bus riders; in 2017 he tried to bar them from stopping at downtown's Public Square.[18] Cleveland's local bus service "is stretched incredibly thin," according to Jarrett Walker, the planner who has helped cities around the globe redo their bus networks. "It's being asked to do too many things with too small a budget."[19]

One of the best examples of how to do things right is Richmond, Virginia. In 2018, the transit agency opened a new rapid bus line, the Pulse, which features bus lanes and off-board fare collection. It simultaneously opened with a redesigned local bus network that focused on simpler routes and higher frequencies.

The Pulse would miss out on some points in the BRT Standard. It doesn't have passing lanes at its stations (3 points) or sliding doors (1 point). But the stat that matters more is that, because Richmond made improvements across the system instead of focusing on one sexy project, bus ridership has increased by 21 percent in just 1 year.[20]

The goal for cities that want to improve buses should be not one beautiful BRT line but a network-wide commitment to making buses faster, more reliable, and convenient to use. Where gold standard features such as dedicated transitways are needed to accomplish that (which are most common in the most congested parts of big cities), cities should build them. Where they aren't, cities shouldn't.

The Fight for Fast Buses

Transit planners and transportation planners now have a toolbox that is bursting with technologies, techniques, and street designs that speed up the bus. But actually getting it done has turned out to be anything but speedy.

The Latin American BRT systems that are so admired by U.S. planners remade huge swathes of their cities. Bogota's TransMilenio opened with 24 miles of BRT routes and has since expanded to 70 miles.

The goal for cities that want to improve buses should be not one beautiful BRT line but a network-wide commitment to making buses faster, more reliable, and convenient to use.

Soon after Chicago mayor Rahm Emanuel took office in 2011, he promised a network of BRT routes across the city; after 7 years, the city had built only 4 miles of bus lanes.[21] Transit planners in Washington, DC have been discussing the need for a bus lane on 16th Street NW since the early years of the Obama administration; a lane may finally appear in 2020.

One contributing factor is that transit agencies often plan modest bus projects as if they were megaprojects, with multiple phases of design and outreach.

These processes can stack the politics against public agencies. They can fail to excite project beneficiaries (few bus riders are excited to hear that the bus might be faster 5 years from now). They often involve several sets of public meetings: the first to talk about what community members experience now, a second set to talk about preliminary recommendations, and more public meetings once the agency has a detailed plan. This is a huge time commitment to ask of the average resident, which means that most people tend to drop in and out, whereas the hardest-core opponents stay involved and continue to complain and raise fears throughout the process.

But cities aren't doomed to slog through. Between 2016 and 2018, municipalities throughout greater Boston piloted several bus lane projects, using an ultra-light, fast "pop-up" model.

These pilots tended to follow a similar pattern. Over the course of a few weeks, city staff banned parking on a short stretch of road for a few hours of the peak commute, used plastic cones or red paint to mark the lane for buses only, and gathered data to see how the trial went.

Everett, a largely working-class municipality of 46,000 residents, was the first to try it, in December 2016. Starting in 2017, the Barr Foundation, a private foundation, helped staff in Cambridge, Watertown, and Arlington follow suit and helped Everett further enhance its bus lane. Somerville launched a pilot lane in 2017, and Boston ran a month-long test in spring 2018, testing out a bus lane in its Roslindale neighborhood to speed up a route that connected to the Orange Line subway.

Universally, the pilots proved popular. The lanes in Boston, Arlington, Somerville, and Everett have all been made permanent. (As of June 2019, Cambridge and Watertown had not decided whether to make permanent their pilot, which involved both municipalities.)

Why did these work? For one, the projects done by the municipalities outside Boston had ironclad backing from local leaders. By 2017, Barr had been advocating for BRT for several years. Mary Skelton Roberts, the co-director of Barr's climate program, and Lisa Jacobson, the mobility program officer, explained to me that the foundation had issued reports, held public events and design competitions, and even taken local officials to experience BRT projects in Mexico City.

Even after all that, the reformers working to bring bus priority to the region perceived little enthusiasm from the city of Boston. An application-based competitive process, then, allowed them to suss out which municipalities might be interested in trying something. "We said, 'should we be looking at the coalition of the willing'?" said Skelton Roberts.

Second, Barr gave the winning municipalities enough planning, public outreach, and communications and design assistance to message the project effectively. This support gave them more ability to reach out to constituents before the pilots launched, document the success of the pilots as they happened, and launch the pilots with eye-catching designs that helped change the public narrative around buses.

Figures 3.3a (left) and 3.3b (right)   The Boston BRT pilot projects included advertising that described bus riders as valued community members. (Images courtesy Barr Foundation.)

It doesn't take a private foundation to provide this type of support; state and regional agencies can give small cities the help they need. The idea for Everett's first pilot, which took place before Barr's competition, came out of a planning report done for the city by the state's transportation department.[22] Richmond signed an agreement with the Virginia Department of Transportation to oversee construction of its Pulse rapid bus line instead of hiring an outside consultant to do so.[23]

Washington, DC's 16th Street NW has been talked about as a candidate for a bus lane since 2008. But it's not quite accurate to say that it's been studied for 10 years. The real problem is that mayoral administrations repeatedly studied the corridor but didn't seriously plan for a bus lane. They had political interest only in smaller solutions such as changes in bus service patterns and optimized signal timing.

When I spoke with Sam Zimbabwe, who was then chief project delivery officer for the District Department of Transportation, and Megan Kanagy, project manager for the most recent study of 16th Street NW, which began in 2015, they expressed a worry that failure could close the door on future bus priority projects.

"I had a concern—and I think others did as well—that we had one more shot to get a good bus lane project," Zimbabwe said. "If we just did something because it was easy, and it was unsuccessful . . . we would set ourselves back again."

This kind of caution slows down projects, but it's often an honest read of political reality. Mayor Emanuel's support for rapid bus projects in Chicago stalled after the third of those projects, on Ashland Avenue, was shelved because of community opposition. The city did not announce another bus priority project for 4 years.

The tactical approach used in greater Boston (and, increasingly, elsewhere) can help create a friendlier politics as well. Tactical projects can begin after short outreach and data collection periods. Municipal staff in Cambridge, Watertown, and Arlington took just a few months to meet with stakeholders. In Everett, the process was even more abbreviated.

"The project was the process," said Jay Monty, Everett's city planner. "We know that 10,000 people a day ride the bus down Broadway [where Everett put its pilot bus lane], and that it's half the mode share during certain times of day," he said. "We don't need much more than that to say that justifies taking parking and prioritizing transit."[24]

The "pop-ups" also immediately demonstrated benefits for thousands of people and built enthusiasm that planners used to make the case for a permanent project. Using data from the Waze traffic app, Arlington planners found that their pop-up bus lane did slow down car traffic, for 1 week; congestion returned to normal after drivers got used to the lane.[25] Bus travel times in the corridor got 40 percent less variable, saving riders 5 minutes on an average trip and 10 minutes on a bad trip. Ninety-five percent of riders surveyed at bus stops said the lane should be made permanent. Surveyors heard reactions like, "All the stress I normally feel about getting on a bus that is immediately clogged in congestion went away."

A tactical approach also helps when advocacy groups have to push local governments over the finish line.

Campaigning for Bus Riders

The City of Boston had created a successful one-day pop-up lane, on Washington Street in its Roslindale neighborhood, in December

Figure 3.4   Bus-only lanes were painted on the street in Cambridge and Watertown as part of a pilot project to improve bus speeds. (Image courtesy Barr Foundation.)

2017. But instead of making it permanent, the city announced it would try another, longer pilot in May 2018. Advocates worried about the city's commitment to speeding up the bus.

Stacy Thompson, executive director of LivableStreets Alliance, a nonprofit advocacy group, believes that the city's caution was rooted in fear of opposition from neighborhood drivers. "I genuinely believe . . . that this was perceived as taking parking away from residents who are in a moderate-income, multilingual, working-class community," she said. "Even though [the city] knew that the bus would serve more people, they were afraid they were going to get this intense community pushback."

In reality, the Metropolitan Area Planning Council, a regional planning group, had found that more than 80 percent of the people parking on Washington Street were from outside the neighborhood.[26] LivableStreets Alliance launched a campaign to simultaneously educate residents and pressure the city to act.

The "pop-ups" also immediately demonstrated benefits for thousands of people and built enthusiasm that planners used to make the case for a permanent project.

"People who live in Roslindale who were [riding] one mile on the bus to get to the Orange Line had to wait 45 minutes," Thompson said. "And then [someone from the suburbs] was driving in, parking in front of their houses, and walking three minutes to the train."

LivableStreets Alliance staff recruited volunteers from the neighborhood to canvass at bus stops, distributing fliers with messages like "Did you know that this bus route carries 19,000 people a day?"

The street team also collected more than 150 stories from riders—nurses, students, and others who were delayed in transit—to share with Boston officials. Asked to characterize them, Thompson laughed. "You know, 'I'm a voter and I can't get to work, Mayor Walsh,' is a good message," she said.

Streetfilms, a national organization that produces videos about sustainable transportation, was also shooting film of the pilot lane. Advocates made it known that the video would be released with either a "happy ending" that lauded the city for making the lane permanent or a cliffhanger that questioned whether the city would send bus riders back into gridlock.

This pressure, and the good results from the pilot, were enough to convince Boston to make the lane permanent. Buses moved about 20 percent faster thanks to the pilot lane, and 94 percent of bus riders and cyclists surveyed during the course of the project called for it to be made permanent.[27] Roslindale community members are now advocating for a lane to go into effect during the evening rush hour as well.[28]

Advocates in Washington were also able to push the city but simply didn't have the same capacity. Coalition for Smarter Growth (CSG), an accomplished organization with a history of shaping regional transportation and development policy, ran several campaigns that helped advance the 16th Street NW project.

According to CSG's policy director, Cheryl Cort, and then–deputy director Aimee Custis (who left CSG after I interviewed her), the organization ran online campaigns, convinced neighborhood commissions along the corridor to issue resolutions in support of the project, and helped bring outside speakers to the District to talk about what rapid bus projects could accomplish.

But CSG was never able to raise enough money to hire more than one staff organizer talking to bus riders. In part this is because it works on a broad array of transportation and land use policy issues in the District, northern Virginia, and suburban Maryland. As of May 2019, the 16th Street bus lane project is just one of twenty campaigns that CSG's five staffers work on.[29]

Both Custis and Cort credited Kishan Putta, a volunteer and neighborhood commission member who made the 16th Street bus lanes his "passion project" and effectively doubled the on-the-ground advocacy presence. But this kind of energy has been missing elsewhere. In 2016, volunteers attempted to organize a Washington Metropolitan Area Transit Authority Transit Riders Union, but the organization flamed out quickly.[30]

District DOT staff felt the gap. "The bus is really the opportunity to make a lot of gains in having an equitable city," Kanagy said. "I think that's where we need advocacy partners, to help tell that story."

Since I first talked with DC transit reformers, there's been a hopeful epilogue. Business leaders have financially backed a new advocacy group, DC Sustainable Transportation. In 2019, mayor Muriel Bowser has endorsed two new bus lane projects, in addition to the 16th Street bus lanes slated for 2020. The two projects are at opposite extremes in terms of cost and timeline. The first is the K Street Transitway, a $122-million BRT-style project that would give over large sections of an eight-lane road to buses instead. The second is a pair of pop-up tactical bus lanes on H and I Streets, two of the busiest streets for bus riders in the District.

Seattle's Transit Reliability Machine

Although most cities in the United States that have high transit use are older cities that developed before mass motorization, Seattle is one of America's modern transit success stories.

Since 2009, the region has operated one of the most successful light rail lines in the country and complemented it with a network of frequent local buses, including six RapidRide lines that have widely spaced stops, sections of bus-only lane, and other elements that provide fast and dependable service. As of 2017, 64 percent of Seattle residents are within a 10-minute walk of transit that runs every 10 minutes or better. Only 25 percent of downtown Seattle commuters drive, and between 2010 and 2016 the downtown added 45,000 jobs with no increase in car traffic.[31]

As of 2017, 64 percent of Seattle residents are within a 10-minute walk of transit that runs every 10 minutes or better.

These outcomes were fought for and won by multiple generations of elected leaders and advocates, which include the Transportation Choices Coalition, which has led multiple ballot measures, strong media outlets such as Seattle Transit Blog, and a wider array of equity-focused and environmental organizations such as Puget Sound Sage and Sightline Institute.

But the region has also been successful in linking political victories to the intentional strengthening of its transportation agencies: the Seattle Department of Transportation (which operates streets in Seattle) and King County Metro (which runs bus service in the county that includes Seattle and thirty-eight other cities and towns). Seattle and King County's transportation agencies have become visionary bureaucracies, with the ability to envisage a transit future for the city and internal structures that churn out transit projects year after year.

In 2006, Seattle voters passed "Bridging the Gap," a 9-year, $544-million property tax levy to fund street and sidewalk projects, including transit enhancements. The same year, voters across King County approved a 0.1 percent sales tax increase that funded two transit "partnership programs."

These were enormous bus-shaped carrots. Under a "service partnership" program, King County Metro offered up tens of thousands of bus service hours that it would provide to any city, employer, or institution willing to cover a third of the cost. And under a "speed and reliability partnership" program, the transit agency agreed to add service on routes where the local government made street changes that reduced bus travel times by up to 10 percent.[32]

Seattle used its "Bridging the Gap" funds to take a big bite of these carrots, buying bus service every year after 2007.[33] The city also created a transit unit within the DOT to determine where that service should go. Seattle DOT's transit work group would go on to build RapidRide lines within the city and worked with King County Metro to determine where extra service hours should go.

In 2014, Seattle voters approved increases in sales tax and vehicle registration fees to buy even more bus service within city limits. Afterward, city leaders reorganized the agency specifically to emphasize transit's importance, according to Bill Bryant, who joined Seattle DOT in 2007. Transit had been handled by a workgroup inside the DOT's policy division, and it was elevated to become its own division, with Bryant as the head of transit capital and service planning.[34] As of 2018, the transit and mobility division now includes twenty-eight positions working on transit capital projects, service planning, and policy.[35]

King County Metro, which runs bus service in Seattle and thirty-eight other cities and towns across the county, also has strong structures. It has a dedicated BRT unit to build out new RapidRide corridors. It also has a novel and long-standing speed and reliability engineering unit, which works on spot improvements across the county.

According to Bryant, who now works as King County Metro's managing director of service development, the speed and reliability group was originally created to make sure municipal street plans could accommodate transit: "How can a bus make this turn?" But as the region has become more committed to transit, the unit has taken a more proactive role, focused on speeding up bus service: "How can a bus get through this intersection first?"

Irin Limargo, the engineer who runs the speed and reliability unit, said that most of the spot improvements her team works on are flagged by bus operators. Twice a year, the unit goes to every depot to meet with bus operators and hear about trouble spots they experience, such as signals that aren't timed well for buses or turns that are hard to make. At any given time, Limargo said, the unit is working on about twenty of these spot improvement projects—with a waitlist of forty to fifty-five spot projects—while also managing three corridor-length projects.

The actual authority for fixing bus slow zones lies with the thirty-nine cities and towns in King County. Other than Seattle and Bellevue (the county's second-largest city), most municipalities have small transportation departments. Limargo's team normally has around nine staffers, all with specialist knowledge of transit. The unit has become something like a medical center of excellence, *the* place in King County that best understands how to engineer streets and signals to keep buses moving through intersections.

Unlike medical specialists, however, the speed and reliability team makes a lot of house calls. It sets up meeting after meeting with local transportation departments, presents them with data on transit ridership and service levels, and offers solutions such as signal or street changes. Limargo described her team members as "plan-gineers" who need to "translate the technical aspect into layperson's terms" so that municipal engineers can explain the need for transit fixes to planners and decisionmakers in their city.

King County Metro has even written a guide for municipal staff, which explains the engineering and design tools that can speed up transit and how the agency prefers to engage with local governments.[36]

We Want a Fast Bus

Delivering public transit is fundamentally a repetitive job. Most mornings in a city, hundreds of bus operators leave their depots to run the same routes they did yesterday. New York City Transit president Andy Byford has compared his job to the movie *Groundhog Day*: "Every day you set out to do the same thing, but you should do it better than the day before."[37]

By streamlining routes and making street improvements, cities can make the complex, chaotic system that is a bus network simpler, faster, and more dependable every day.

Winning these improvements requires transit reformers to understand a pair of chaotic human systems: the politics of projects and the inner workings of public agencies. When advocates and public leaders master the first, they can win bus improvements quickly and broadly. Early success can get politicians hungry for more. In Everett and Somerville, mayors almost immediately started talking about what streets should be next for bus lanes.[38] Boston committed to launching two new pop-up lanes in 2019, in the Allston and Charlestown neighborhoods, and is planning a third in Mattapan.[39]

By streamlining routes and making street improvements, cities can make the complex, chaotic system that is a bus network simpler, faster, and more dependable every day.

In the long run, they can embed transit improvement machines within the bureaucracy that deliver a continuous stream of transit fixes. Boston, which advocates initially viewed as lukewarm toward bus priority, is now institutionalizing it. In 2018, the Boston Transportation Department announced it would create its first-ever "transit team," a five-person unit that will manage and implement transit priority projects.[40]

As urban traffic continues to worsen, cities need to design streets, draw routes, and structure organizations to provide fast and dependable transit.

"We're creating this circle where we provide good service, people appreciate it and they demand it, and so we have to provide it and keep improving it," Bryant said. "The competition . . . the single occupant vehicle and Uber and Lyft . . . is getting better and better. We have to keep up with that competition, and in order to do that, this circle needs to continue to accelerate and expand."

04 MAKE THE BUS WALKABLE AND DIGNIFIED

—

On a Saturday afternoon in April 2010, Raquel Nelson, her 4-year-old son A.J., and her two other children (aged 2 and 9 years) stepped off the bus across the street from their apartment in Marietta, Georgia. It had been a good but long day. Raquel and her children had celebrated a birthday with family and pizza. To get home, they took their first bus from the pizza restaurant to a transit center, where they missed their connecting bus and had to wait more than an hour for the next one.

Home was across a five-lane, divided road. And so, together with several other people who had been on the bus, the Nelson family crossed halfway across the street to wait in the median. As Raquel stopped to gauge traffic, one of the other adults in the group decided to start walking. Raquel's son A.J. broke free from her grip to follow, and Raquel hurried to catch up.

A.J. was killed moments later, by Jerry Guy, who was behind the wheel of a van despite having "three or four beers" in his system.[1] Raquel and her 2-year-old daughter were also struck and injured. And yet that was only the beginning of her ordeal.

County prosecutors charged Raquel with vehicular homicide, which carried a potential sentence of 3 years in prison. A jury convicted her, and she was sentenced to 12 months' probation with the option of a retrial, which she chose. Her case wound through the courts for 2 more years before Raquel agreed to plead guilty to a single charge of jaywalking.

Raquel Nelson's case made national news. But the loss she and her family experienced is replicated in nearly every city on wide "arterial" roads that encourage high speeds. In the City of Los Angeles, for example, 6 percent of streets are responsible for 65 percent of traffic deaths and injuries.[2] When mapped, pedestrian deaths line up on these roads like dominoes.

Because they tend to have important destinations on them, arterial roads also tend to carry the most bus riders. But the tie between transit and walkability goes beyond pedestrian safety. Nearly all transit riders are pedestrians at some point during their trip. In Los Angeles, for example, 84 percent of bus riders get to their bus stop on foot.[3]

The pedestrian experience *is* the transit experience, then. A bus rider may appreciate frequent and fast service but still be dissatisfied with her trip if she has to trudge through mud on the way to the bus stop, cross the street with her head on a swivel, and wait in the rain with no shelter. Someone who uses a wheelchair may be unable to use the bus at all if there are no sidewalks leading to the stop.

Poor walkability is corrosive to bus ridership and makes it harder to improve transit service. In Staten Island, New York City, transit planners had to make major adjustments to a redesign of the borough's express buses after riders complained that the changes forced them to walk in the street or on lawns.[4]

Although Austin's bus network redesign has generally been considered a success, it ran into the same problems. More than a month after the launch of the redesign, Capital Metro was still moving stop locations in response to complaints that people had to transfer in places without good walking infrastructure. "If you're going to go to more of a grid-based system and you're going to have more on-street connections, then you really need to look at the pedestrian experience of those intersections," Capital Metro's Todd Hemingson said.[5] (As of April 2019, only about 60 percent of streets in Austin have sidewalks.[6])

Improving the walk to transit, on the other hand, can have measurable impacts on transit ridership. Ja Young Kim, Keith Bartholomew, and Reid Ewing of the University of Utah found that after the Utah Transit Authority built sidewalk connections to bus stops that lacked them, ridership at those stops grew almost twice as fast as at stops in similar neighborhoods that had not been improved. Demand for paratransit was also stemmed near the stops with sidewalk improvements, saving the agency on its budget.[7]

Although walkability and transit can't be separated, government usually makes its best effort to do so. Just as transit agencies must convince cities to give transit priority on the street, they must rely on local and state government to create a good walking environment. That's no given.

Fixing Walkability

The state of walking in America represents an enormous collective failure. Even in urban neighborhoods where many people walk, engineering practices that favor drivers tend to degrade the experience. Intersections can be designed with slip lanes that allow cars to gun through turns. Zoning may allow curb cuts that turn the sidewalk into a gauntlet of traffic. The default rule at most intersections is "right turn on red," intrinsically hostile to people walking because there's never a time when they can be sure cars won't turn into their path.

Poor walkability is corrosive to bus ridership and makes it harder to improve transit service. Improving the walk to transit, on the other hand, can have measureable impacts on ridership.

These decisions are rooted in a philosophy that prioritizes vehicle speeds and is often baked into engineering measures and practices. Engineers often assess streets using a metric called "automobile level of service," where an A grade is free-flowing traffic. A major traffic engineering manual recommends against striping crosswalks unless at least ninety-three pedestrians already cross the intersection per hour—or if five people were hit by cars at the intersection in the past year.[8] Peter Furth, an engineering professor at Northeastern University, has pointed out that "Synchro, the standard software [traffic engineers] use, is based on minimizing auto delay, and it doesn't even calculate pedestrian delay."[9]

Although most streets are municipally maintained, most cities require local property owners to maintain sidewalks abutting their property. This means that wealthier neighborhoods tend to have better maintained and safer sidewalks. The further you get from downtown, the more likely it is that sidewalks themselves will shrink, decay, or vanish. Property owners may not be required to build sidewalks at all, which means many cities simply lack sidewalks in a huge portion of their territory.

For example, in 2017 the city of Denver found that 40 percent of streets were missing sidewalks or had sidewalks that were too narrow for people using wheelchairs.[10] This was true near transit as well: Of sidewalks within a half-mile of light rail stops or a quarter-mile of bus stops and bike share stations, 39 percent were missing or too narrow. Completing Denver's sidewalk network will cost at least $800 million and as much as $1.4 billion (for wider, more functional sidewalks). When the report came out, Denver was budgeting less than $20 million a year for sidewalk and curb ramp improvements, and it is still struggling to increase that amount.

The state of walking in America represents an enormous collective failure. Even in urban neighborhoods where many people walk, engineering practices that favor drivers tend to degrade the experience.

Houston allows many property owners to veto construction of sidewalks when their street gets rebuilt. Property owners on streets without sidewalks can request them from the city, but this takes 3 to 5 years. The city's budget for new sidewalks is $2.6 million, but as of December 2018 there was a backlog of 580 requests, costing $83 million.[11] The city has no inventory of the condition of existing sidewalks.

Fixing walkability is a problem large enough to be the subject of its own book (actually, it's the subject of two: Jeff Speck's *Walkable City* and *Walkable City Rules*). What, if anything, can transit agencies do to address the problem?

How Transit Agencies Can Lead

Transit agencies have to treat pedestrian access like the critical factor it is, not ignore it because it's typically outside their jurisdiction. Where they can, they should pay for walking connections themselves. Measure M, which increased sales tax in the Los Angeles region in 2016 to fund transportation projects, includes a small portion dedicated to "first mile/last mile" improvements; Los Angeles Metro uses it to run a program aimed at fixing pedestrian connections to transit.

They can also make sure that when they collaborate with cities on projects aimed at improving bus speeds, they put pedestrian fixes on the agenda. Nearly all of the Select Bus Service projects implemented by New York City Transit and the city's Department of Transportation include elements that create a better walk, such as pedestrian refuge islands and sidewalk "bulb-outs" at bus stops.

When opportunities like these aren't available, transit agencies can use data to help municipalities understand the issue. TriMet, the transit operator for the Portland region, completed a pedestrian network analysis in 2012 where it analyzed 7,000 of its bus stops to find areas where walking connections to transit were poor, but there was high potential for transit ridership (based on surrounding density, transit ridership, and destinations such as schools and senior housing).[12] It identified ten "focus areas" for intervention and has convinced several cities to pour new sidewalks and design safer crossings.

There's one more element to think about: Are the bus stops themselves worth walking to and waiting at?

Shelters: The Front Door to Transit

It's a sign of the fundamental brokenness of the American healthcare system that many people turn to GoFundMe and other fundraising platforms to pay for medical bills. In the world of transit, a similarly troubling do-it-yourself system has sprung up to give bus riders a place to sit.

In 2014, the advocacy group Ride New Orleans put 200 folding chairs on downtown sidewalks, at an intersection that is a major bus transfer point.[13] Activists with Cincinnati's Better Bus Coalition put together blue wooden benches in a wood shop and drop them off at bus stops.[14] In Los Angeles, a single anonymous artist has installed a dozen benches on the city's Eastside.[15] In Atlanta, so many bus stops were missing schedule information (and even the numbers of the route that stopped there) that volunteer "soldiers" from the advocacy group MARTA Army began adopting stops, printing and laminating signs with bus information, and attaching them to nearby poles and fences.

The provision of shelters is key to making transit feel dignified. There is something fundamentally undignified about waiting for the bus on the side of the road, sometimes on the shoulder or a patch of grass. When I've done it, I've felt exposed, as if I'd accidentally shown up in a T-shirt to a formal party.

And that's in good weather. People traveling in cars are shielded from the rain, snow, and hot sun (and most profoundly, shielded from harm by seat belts, air bags, and crumple zones). What a clear statement of disrespect, then, that people waiting for buses so often must do so with neither shade nor shelter, without even a seat or a garbage receptacle, and often without a safe way to walk to the stop.

Through a remarkably clever experiment, three University of Minnesota researchers (Yingling Fan, Andrew Guthrie, and David Levinson) have quantified this psychological toll. Research assistants surreptitiously filmed people as they waited at bus stops in the Twin Cities. Once those people boarded the bus, another set of research assistants surveyed them, asking how long they thought they had waited for the bus.

By comparing the objective reality caught on film with the subjective reality in riders' heads, Fan, Guthrie, and Levinson discovered that bus stop amenities make a huge difference. When riders were waiting at a naked bus stop, with just a sign on a pole, they reported that a wait of just 2 and a half minutes felt like 8. A 10-minute wait

Figure 4.1   People seek shade behind a tree while waiting for a bus in Los Angeles. (Image courtesy Outfront/Decaux.)

felt like it took 21 minutes. The wait felt even longer for women waiting in neighborhoods they thought were unsafe.[16]

When riders had a bench, shelter, and countdown clock at their bus stop, this "time penalty" almost completely disappeared (in neighborhoods perceived as safe). A bench alone was enough to significantly cut perceived waiting time.

Seating is more than a mere amenity. Berry Farrington, a planner for Metro Transit in the Twin Cities, recalls how a board member of the Highrise Representative Council, which represents residents of public housing, explained the importance of benches. What the board member heard from some older residents, Farrington said, was, "If I've walked a quarter-mile to a bus stop, I physically cannot stand there and wait for the bus. I can't make that walk if I can't sit down."

In other words, seating itself enables access to transit. "If we can make a bus stop environment that allows someone the convenience of regular route bus service, that's pretty important to know," Farrington said.

Improving conditions at bus stops is worth doing on its own, but it's also a logical complement to efforts to speed up and redesign bus service. Bus routes should have fewer stops, but the stops that remain should be dignified places to wait. Adding shelters should go hand in hand with stop consolidation.

Yet despite their importance, shelters are often relegated to a bureaucratic no-man's-land that leaves them an afterthought. Depending on the municipality, the authority to place a bus shelter may rest with the local transportation department, a city councilmember, or even a private advertising company.[17]

In larger cities, bus shelters are often a good base for advertising. This can be a good thing, especially if the money is used as a revenue stream for shelter maintenance rather than a city's general fund. The value of advertising varies significantly by market; a 2013 review found that a single ad could bring in anywhere from $150 to $4,500 for a 4-week period.[18] But these benefits aren't worth it if the contract is written in a way that gives the advertising company total control over where shelters are placed. This is a recipe to concentrate shelters where its ads get the best views, such as a downtown shopping district, instead of where they are most needed.

Figure 4.2   Bus stops that don't warrant or cannot fit shelters can still be improved through seating. This TriMet bus stop has seating built into the stop pole. (Image courtesy J. Daniel Malouff.)

In many cities, the location of bus shelters has been determined by the same force that has determined the shape of bus routes: an ad hoc combination of history and complaint. The New York City DOT, which is in charge of bus shelters in New York, effectively administers its contract with the advertiser that builds and maintains shelters; shelters have been replaced even faster than the contract demands. But the department has essentially no guidelines for which stops should get shelters, instead consulting with local elected officials and community boards.

This squeaky-wheel approach rewards the connected, not the deserving. Instead, agencies must develop clear, logical rules to determine where shelters go—for example, at bus stops where many people board, where many people transfer, where there are large numbers of wheelchair users, and near certain key destinations, such as senior housing and hospitals.

Shelter placement is also hamstrung when each shelter needs a separate approval. This invites petty meddling by businesses or homeowners who don't want bus riders congregating near them. In September 2018, New York City councilmember Jumaane Williams held up an entire rapid bus project, the B82 Select Bus Service in Brooklyn, because he claimed there had not been sufficient public outreach. It turned out that he was responding to complaints from a homeowner who opposed a bus stop in front of his building.[19]

The City of Los Angeles has perhaps the clearest example of an approval process that was designed to fail. Placing a single bus shelter within city limits requires sign-off from nine different entities: the local councilmember; the city bureaus of Street Services, Engineering, Street Lighting, and Contract Administration; its departments of Planning, Public Works, and Transportation; and the city police department. If adjacent property owners object to a shelter, yet another agency, the Board of Public Works, is responsible for resolving the complaint. In 2012, the city controller found that approving a shelter and issuing a construction permit took, on average, 4 months.[20]

Bus shelters were an innocent victim of legislative crossfire. When city councilors drafted a law regulating shelters, they classified them as "street furniture," just like newsstands and public toilets. The toilets set off enormous controversy, resulting in a stringent approval process for all street furniture, including bus shelters.

Instead, cities should grant, and public transit agencies should seek, a blanket permit that gives the agency the authority to site shelters at any stop, perhaps subject to some objective criteria.

Many of these lessons can be illustrated by the experience of Metro Transit, in Minneapolis–St. Paul, which recently went through a process that transformed how its staff thought about bus shelters and how they related to the riders that use them.

Metro Transit's Better Bus Stops Program

Metro Transit's Better Bus Stops program was designed to reme-
diate a status quo that had come to reflect inequities in the region
it served. Suburban bus stops were supposed to get shelters if they
served at least twenty-five boardings a day; city stops had to meet
a higher standard of forty.[21] Shelters were sometimes placed reac-
tively, in response to customer complaints.

A 2014 investigation by the *Star-Tribune* found that 460 bus stops
met the agency's criteria for shelters but didn't have them.[22] Meanwhile, 200 of the agency's 801 shelters were at stops that didn't have
enough ridership to justify them (69 of those were inherited from a
private advertiser after Metro Transit took over administration of
shelters in Minneapolis).

---

*In many cities, the location of bus shelters has
been determined by the same force that has
determined the shape of bus routes: an ad hoc
combination of history and complaint.*

The investigation came out at a time when community, faith-
based, and philanthropic groups had succeeded in raising racial and
social equity as an issue in local politics. Minneapolis mayor Betsy
Hodges took office after campaigning on closing racial disparities
in the city. The Metropolitan Council, the regional government that
oversees Metro Transit, released a blockbuster report that found
that the Twin Cities had "some of the nation's biggest disparities
along racial and ethnic lines among our peer metro cities." White
residents in the region had an average income of $38,000, compared
with $18,000 for residents of color.[23]

These forces came to a head in 2014, as the agency was planning
to extend its Green Line light rail from Minneapolis through several of its southwestern suburbs. A group of thirty regional, local,
and neighborhood organizations, under the banner of the Equity
Commitments Coalition for Southwest Light Rail, called on Metro
Transit to plan bus connections with rail, integrate it with affordable housing, improve bike and pedestrian connections, and add bus

shelters. Farrington recalls that the sentiment was, "You're going to add this great rail station out in an affluent city, but what about my bus stop at school, too?"

Minneapolis sided with the advocates, saying it would not approve the planned route of the rail line unless Metro Transit built additional bus shelters in some of its poorest neighborhoods. (State law required Metro Transit to get consent from each of the municipalities the rail line would run through.)

To its advantage, Metro Transit has almost sole responsibility for siting bus shelters. It agreed to the conditions set by the city and saw an opportunity to go further by using a $3.26-million grant from the Federal Transit Administration's "Ladders of Opportunity" initiative, a priority of Obama administration transportation secretary Anthony Foxx.

The goal of the project was to add 150 shelters, and add heat, light, or both to seventy-five, in "racially concentrated areas of poverty," low-income neighborhoods where more than half of residents were nonwhite. This meant twenty-eight neighborhoods in Minneapolis, nine in St. Paul, and parts of three suburbs (Brooklyn Center, Brooklyn Park, and Richfield) that fit that description. The other goal was to rethink the whole process of siting shelters, informed by the voices of riders themselves.

Metro Transit applied for the grant with the intention of reserving 10 percent for public engagement and making sure engagement was part of the project from the beginning. Ultimately, the agency spent about $87,000 for engagement across its service area and dedicated another $332,000 for engagement in the target neighborhoods.

This neighborhood funding went to a "community engagement team" of two nonprofits (the Alliance for Metropolitan Stability and Nexus Community Partners) and the Center for Urban and Regional Affairs at the University of Minnesota. These groups had a track record from the Corridors of Opportunity Project, an earlier partnership that supported equitable development around planned light rail expansions.

The engagement team was responsible for hiring groups to do the frontline work with transit riders. Their request for proposals was purposely open to different styles of engagement, and they invited additional community organizations to help judge the applicants.

"Creating the conditions where [community organizations] could bring their own local expertise and relationships into this process was really important," said Caitlin Schwartz, who was a community outreach coordinator for Metro Transit (she now consults for Nexus Community Partners). "In the public sector there's a pretty established process of making people come to you, doing open houses and, you know, scratching your heads: 'Why didn't anyone show up to this open house?' This really flipped that. Both we as staff and our partners really went to people, and we established a process to foster that."

Ultimately, the engagement team ended up hiring eleven community groups on contracts of $15,000 to $25,000. These included neighborhood organizations (such as the Harrison and Nokomis East Neighborhood Associations), a transportation-focused group (St. Paul Smart Trips), a business group (West Broadway Business & Area Coalition), and a group that represented public housing residents (the Highrise Representative Council). The subcontractors received mentorship and training from the engagement team and regularly met as a group to compare notes and learn from each other.

Their task was to ask residents where shelters were most needed, which bus stop features were most important, how the design of bus stops affected their experience, which historic places in the neighborhood might need contextually sensitive designs, and broader issues that affected transit equity in the region. Their methods varied substantially by organization. Some groups knocked on residents' doors, others surveyed riders as they rode the bus, and others tabled at schools and community centers. Ultimately, Metro Transit and the community groups engaged more than 7,000 people, including at 185 community events. They also got back 2,013 completed surveys.[24]

One proof of the process is in those results. Bus riders are disproportionately immigrants and people with low income, both groups that tend to be underrepresented in surveys. But the Better Bus Stops survey respondents did reflect the age, gender, ethnicity, and race of Metro Transit's bus riders. More than a third of respondents were people of color, and more than a third did not have access to a car. Twenty percent indicated having a disability. More than half of survey responses came from the community organizations subcontracted by Metro Transit.

Respondents identified the separate rules for the suburbs and the cities as inherently unfair. They also said that a simple rule based on ridership didn't capture their values; shelter placement, they thought, should be responsive to particularly vulnerable riders such as seniors, people with disabilities, and people getting medical treatment.

As a result, the agency rewrote its guidelines for placing shelters. The new criteria do away with separate rules and weigh two factors: how well used the bus stop is and whether it is in a "priority location," that is, in a neighborhood with many carless households; near healthcare, social service facilities, or housing for older adults or people with disabilities; or at a major transfer point.[25]

Metro Transit Shelter Siting Criteria (adapted from agency guidelines)

Shelter Improvement	Criteria
Highest priority for adding a shelter	100+ daily boardings at stop in a "priority location" (area where many households do not own a car; near hospitals, healthcare clinics, social service providers, housing for people with disabilities or older adults; and major transfer points)
High priority for adding a shelter	100+ daily boardings at stop
Medium priority for adding a shelter	30+ daily boardings at stop in a "priority location"
Lower priority for adding a shelter	30+ daily boardings at stop
Replace existing shelter when needed	15+ daily boardings at stop
Remove existing shelter	<15 daily boardings at stop
Add light to shelter	Prioritized based on number of boardings during "dark hours," documented personal security concerns, access to electricity, and quality of other area lighting (e.g., streetlamps); not a standard shelter feature
Add heat to shelter	100+ daily boardings at stop, if there is cost-effective access to electricity; not a standard shelter feature

The agency also heard fine-grained feedback on the importance of seating, heat, and light. It even learned that it could do a better job of placing shelters.

Before the Better Bus Stops program, Farrington said, "our biggest shelter was thought of as the 'Cadillac of shelters'; [the philosophy was] we should always put that shelter wherever we can."

Riders didn't always feel like that gave them a Cadillac experience. "We were squeezing these really big shelters into spaces where they *technically* fit, but it wasn't great," Farrington said. "Especially for the ADA community, [we were] just putting an obstacle in the pedestrian path." Now, the agency has a standard "slim shelter" for constrained locations.

A simple rule based on ridership didn't capture their values; shelter placement, they thought, should be responsive to particularly vulnerable riders such as seniors, people with disabilities, and people getting medical treatment.

In general, Farrington said, "there's a much higher level of attention placed to design." Every planned bus shelter now has an engineering drawing made of it. This drawing gets circulated within Metro Transit (for example, to the bus operations team, which might recognize that a proposed shelter is too close to the curb for comfort) and with local municipalities.

Metro Transit also began building out its internal systems for tracking shelters. The legacy database that tracks where shelters are currently placed doesn't give Metro Transit the ability to do two things Farrington would like it to. It can't analyze how shelter placements are doing against the agency's goals for equitable shelter placement. It also doesn't sync with the agency's work orders; if it did, the agency would be able to see at a glance when shelters were last cleaned and maintained and know whether certain shelters received more maintenance than others.

A new data support tool, built with open-source software, may allow the agency to see at a glance which stops should have shelters based on the new guidelines (based on ridership and land use, such as whether the stop is near a hospital), as well as stops where shelters should be removed. Internally, the agency has also developed an equity performance metric to determine whether the percentage of customer boardings at stops with shelters is equal systemwide and in census blocks that are predominantly low-income and communities of color.[26]

Metro Transit is on track to meet its goal of installing 150 shelters in priority neighborhoods in 2019. As of December 2018, 64 percent of boardings in racially concentrated areas of poverty take place at a sheltered bus stop, similar to the systemwide average, according to Farrington.

Fighting for People on Foot

Pedestrian infrastructure doesn't cost much relative to other transportation infrastructure. Houston's $83 million in backlogged sidewalk requests could mostly be wiped out by nixing a $70 million project to add an interchange on an area toll road.[27] Even the $1.4-billion price tag to build functional sidewalk on every Denver street doesn't look so daunting when the Colorado Department of Transportation is spending $1.2 billion in just 4 years to widen Interstate 70, which runs northeast of downtown Denver.[28]

Shelters aren't particularly expensive either, costing roughly between $5,500 and $12,000 each.[29] In 2017, medium and large transit agencies spent $297 million on infrastructure at bus stops and stations, compared with $2.2 billion on rail stations—or about 6 cents per bus trip and 47 cents per rail trip.[30]

Creating walkable places requires changing municipal processes so that compact planning (creating neighborhoods where there are many destinations worth walking to) and pedestrian-friendly street design become routine.

This often starts with outside advocacy and political action.

The do-it-yourself movements I mentioned earlier in this chapter ultimately seek not to supplant government but to prod it to action. A year after MARTA Army launched its "adopt-a-stop" campaign, the state of Georgia awarded the Atlanta Regional Commission $3.8 million for bus stop signs, shelters, and sidewalks.[31] Cincinnati's Better Bus Coalition doesn't just build benches; it has also published an analysis showing that shelters are disproportionately in wealthy neighborhoods.[32] *Streetsblog USA* runs an annual "Sorriest Bus Stop in America" contest that has gotten governments in Kansas City, Maryland, and Boston to address bus stop walkability.

In Nashville, a long-time neighborhood activist, Angie Henderson, was elected to the city's Metropolitan Council on a platform of walkable neighborhoods in 2015.[33] Henderson later sponsored and passed a law requiring most developments in inner-city neighborhoods and near commercial centers to include sidewalks or pay into a citywide sidewalk fund.[34] Denver's City Council created a $4 million fund to help lower-income homeowners fix the sidewalks in front of their houses and budgeted for three new Public Works employees to manage the program and step up enforcement of sidewalk regulations throughout the city. And Seattle's Department of Transportation has broken with the engineering guideline that says crosswalks should be striped only where many people already cross or where there are frequent pedestrian crashes.

Pedestrian infrastructure doesn't cost much relative to other transportation infrastructure.

Within transit agencies themselves, it's important to raise the profile of the walk and the wait. Metro Transit's Better Bus Stops Program is a great example. The decision to elevate a routine process into a branded program gave bus stops new stature throughout the agency.

"[The process of citing bus shelters] could be thought of as very dull and unimportant," Farrington said. "But to package it, to get a great little logo and have it be a substantial program with its own name and people, it's been a positive spiral of more resources and more support of the work." She said that staff who had previously worked on park-and-ride stations were now spending more time on bus stops.

True, in some ways the program was an outlier, funded by an Obama-era discretionary program, Ladders of Opportunity, that no longer exists. But transit agencies could replicate it using funding from many other sources.

Metro Transit's program also offers a clear example of how well-resourced, well-planned public engagement can strengthen and educate both the transit agency and the communities it operates in.

This started by hiring local groups with neighborhood ties. Funding for outreach means "we don't exhaust our resources or burn out our volunteers," Denetrick Powers, a former organizer for the Harrison Neighborhood Association, told the website Streets.mn. "It gives us an opportunity to give back to our residents, to pay them—they need to be paid. It helps us to do the work we want to do. It also helps us build relationships with the community."[35]

The community groups that were contracted to work grew stronger through the process. After the project ended, the Harrison Neighborhood Association decided to keep several of its transit organizers on the payroll to do voter organizing. One of the Corcoran Neighborhood Organization's volunteer leaders was named to the group's board.[36]

Schwartz said, "A lot of public agencies have really extractive relationships with communities; I've been in a lot of workshops with agencies who talk about 'community' as the necessary evil of the work, checking the box of what they feel like they have to do."

What the Better Bus Stops project represents, at least in a small way, is a process that did more than simply take advantage of local knowledge and capacity to garner political cover for the agency. Instead, it grew the capacity of local institutions as it advanced.

Working with small organizations can be challenging; one of the eleven subcontracted groups was unable to complete the work because of staff turnover. But the point of the project was to help low-resource neighborhoods. Nurturing the human capital and institutions in those neighborhoods—building their social infrastructure in tandem with the physical—gives Metro Transit potential future allies and gives people in those neighborhoods more power to advocate for their needs in the future.

It's worth recalling, though, that the Better Bus Stops program came about in the context of a much larger discussion of resources. Is a few million dollars for bus stops a fair trade for a $2 billion suburban light rail project? These questions of equity and resources are at the heart of transit planning.

05 MAKE THE BUS FAIR AND WELCOMING

—

Bus service shapes the geography of accessibility, and this means how we plan bus service is deeply intertwined with social equity, whether we admit it or not. Transit agencies are required by federal law to analyze whether fare and service changes disproportionately harm low-income riders and riders of color, but this is often performed as a check-the-box exercise. Planning in ways that intentionally advance social equity requires a deeper commitment from transit leaders.

Because bus riders in the United States are more likely to be low income and nonwhite, some argue that advocating for better buses is, by definition, advocating for more equitable transit. But this syllogism, never wholly true, is even less so if we fail to consider questions about the affordability of transit and who feels welcome on transit.

For example, an increased police presence on buses can make some riders feel safer while discomfiting and endangering others. New fare systems can make transit more intuitive and convenient for many riders while being rolled out in ways that worsen transit access for others.

Buses provide spatial access but are also public spaces themselves. How transit agencies seek to ensure safety for bus riders, how they charge for access, and who the service feels intuitive for affects which riders feel welcome on the bus and which are excluded.

Planning with an Equity Lens

Federal law supposedly safeguards the rights of low-income and minority transit riders; Title VI of the Civil Rights Act of 1964 states that no one in the United States "shall, on the ground of race, color, or national origin, be excluded from participation in, be denied the benefits of, or be subjected to discrimination" under programs that receive federal funds; this includes public transit, because virtually all transit agencies receive some federal funding.

Unfortunately, enforcing these rights relies on an administrative process that is so open to interpretation that transit agencies can easily push through inequitable service changes.[1]

Before we go further, a note on the word *equity*: When I use it, I mean policies that reduce the burdens and mitigate the structural pains put on marginalized communities. I'm talking about transit policies that particularly improve access for, and reduce harm to, racial and ethnic minorities, non–English speakers, women, people with disabilities, and low-income people, whose needs are not centered in public policy. *Equity* is often used in other ways in the transportation policy world. Legislators often talk about "regional equity," or whether they perceive that their jurisdiction gets the service it deserves based on how much tax it pays. But the way I use the term is increasingly the common usage in urban policy.

Equity: *policies that reduce the burdens and mitigate the structural pains put on marginalized communities.*

Federal regulations require transit agencies to analyze fare changes and major service changes and determine whether they have "disparate impact" on communities of color. But just as Hollywood accountants deny actors their residuals by claiming that the *Star Wars* and *Harry Potter* films have actually lost money, transit agencies have so much leeway in applying Title VI that almost no inequity gets labeled a violation.[2]

For example, agencies themselves define what level of service change qualifies as "major." If they want to cut service on a route, they can decide to analyze either the riders who use the route or the people who live near the route. (Imagine a bus line carrying low-income Hispanic riders through a wealthy white neighborhood. Cutting the line looks inequitable if the agency focuses on the Hispanic people who ride the bus but might not be considered a violation in an analysis that focuses on the white neighborhood the bus runs through.)

Alex Karner, a professor at the University of Texas in Austin, has pointed out that a city could get rid of all of its bus service without running afoul of Title VI. There wouldn't be a "disparate impact"—both white and nonwhite bus riders would get the same 100 percent service cut![3]

Furthermore, even if a service or fare change is deemed to have "disparate impact" on people of color, transit agencies don't necessarily have to remedy it. Instead, they can convince the Federal Transit Administration (FTA) that the change is the "least discriminatory alternative" available.

The Civil Rights Act, then, has been unable to guarantee the right to mobility. In the words of Shawn Fleek, director of narrative strategy at OPAL Environmental Justice, a Portland advocacy group, seeking redress through Title VI is a "tactic, one particular way in which we can address equity issues . . . and the threat of that tool is, I think, probably more effective than its actual use."

It is up to localities to seek fairer transit outcomes. As Hayley Richardson and I wrote in *Governing*, "transit equity starts at home, not in Washington."[4]

San Francisco's Municipal Transportation Authority (SFMTA), for example, adopted a "service equity strategy" in 2018. It prioritizes increased frequency and speed improvements on transit routes that serve many seniors and disabled people and that serve neighborhoods with racially concentrated poverty.

Politicians sometimes complain that they don't know what equity means. The SFMTA makes it very clear: Advancing equity means bigger buses on the 9R route in the Mission, actively managing headways on Chinatown's 10 route, and more service on the 44 in Bayview.[5]

Getting to this level of clarity is hard for most transit agencies, because equitable transit investment requires equitable politics. In the Bay Area, it took years of organizing by advocacy and social justice groups such as Urban Habitat and Public Advocates to win the commitment to the service equity strategy, and then additional consultation with advocates to help draft the content of the strategy itself.

More typical is the kind of uproar touched off in 2014 when the Metropolitan Council, the Twin Cities regional government, changed how it scored transportation investments so that more points were given to projects that would benefit racially concentrated areas of poverty. These were modest changes, affecting up to 3 percent of a road project's score and 12 percent of a transit project's score. A newspaper investigation later found the changes had significantly affected the ranking of fewer than 6 percent of projects, which included two service increases on Minneapolis bus routes.[6] But suburban leaders have cried foul, decrying the focus on equity as "social engineering" and "favoritism," and resisting further changes. An Equity Advisory Committee created by the council has spent most of its time talking about process issues, not providing meaningful input into project selection, according to committee members.[7]

Safety on Transit

During focus groups, you often hear testimony that sticks in your mind long after. One outlier, for me, was a woman who had seen a fatal shooting on a bus in a California city. That was enough to keep her from using transit for a few years. She started riding again after moving to the Pacific Northwest, but her partner was assaulted while riding. Somehow, this series of events hadn't dulled her affection for the bus. She was one of the most pro-transit voices in the focus groups; she even described riding transit, and paying higher taxes to fund it, as a civic duty.

Not everyone is so dedicated in the face of danger. In a 2016 survey, Los Angeles Metro found that nearly a third of former transit riders stopped riding because of safety concerns or discomfort.[8]

"Transit equity starts at home, not in Washington."

Where there's an actual crime problem, police deployment can make a difference. In 2013, Detroit bus operators went on strike to protest what they viewed as unacceptable levels of assault and harassment on board. Over the next 3 years the city expanded the transit police force to forty-three officers, allowing officers to randomly board buses more often and to respond more quickly when incidents occurred.[9] The local transit union president, Fred Westbrook, and some riders, such as 16-year-old Jemirah Edison and 48-year-old Joe Lopez, were supportive of the changes, which cut average police response time from 20 minutes to 10.

But adding more police to transit makes other transit riders feel less safe and puts them at risk of being brutalized. In an ideal world, we'd have demilitarized police who are trained in de-escalation techniques and who know how to approach people suffering mental health episodes. In reality, we have a well-documented problem of cops who use violence to enforce obedience.

Orlando Lopez, a bus rider organizer at OPAL, said it's important to ask the most vulnerable riders what safety means to them. OPAL, a membership-based environmental justice group that organizes low-income people and people of color, has been doing that since 2006.

In 2017, for example, OPAL convened community forums after a high-profile attack on the Portland light rail system, when a white supremacist harassed two women of color and then stabbed three people who tried to intervene, two fatally.

The transit agency's response was to increase police, but OPAL members argued that this would only lead to more fare inspection sweeps. The organization held three public forums under the theme of "What Is Safety?" According to Lopez and Fleek, what they heard from those discussions was that "community-defined safety" would address feelings that riders had about being harassed by police, fare inspectors, or bus operators; lack of safe pedestrian crossings; and the feeling of exposure as bus riders waited at unlit, unsheltered bus stops in the dark.

Rather than increase police, OPAL has called on TriMet to revive a program from the 1990s known as the "rider ambassadors," contracted staff who live in or have connections to the neighborhoods they are based in, who are trained in the use of de-escalation techniques to defuse disputes on transit.

I don't believe there is a one-size-fits-all answer when it comes to safety on transit. But it is worth noting that transportation research has found only a weak relationship between actual transit crime rates and how safe people say they feel while waiting for transit. A study from Australia's University of Monash found that whether someone feels comfortable traveling with strangers does more to predict whether they feel unsafe on transit than whether they had been personally attacked or threatened or seen someone attacked or threatened.[10]

Media stories about disorder on transit have also been linked to perceptions that the system is unsafe.[11] This includes social media. In a 2018 focus group that I observed in Philadelphia, several transit riders said that videos of Philadelphia "transit craziness" were readily available on YouTube. Seeing these videos, one woman said, was the reason why she didn't ride the bus.[12]

A substantial body of research has found that the design of transit facilities and the characteristics of neighborhoods that transit sits in play a role in feelings of safety. UCLA's Anastasia Loukaitou and Camille Fink have found that darkness and desolation make people feel less secure; so do transit facilities that cut off people's line of sight.[13]

A substantial body of research has found that the design of transit facilities and the characteristics of neighborhoods that transit sits in play a role in feelings of safety.

Because bus riders' perception of safety has so much to do with the physical and informational environment, transit agencies need to think beyond the bus. According to Loukaitou and Fink, riders report feeling less anxious about safety when they're on the bus and more anxious while walking to or waiting at the stop. (This suggests, by the way, that running service more often should improve perceptions of safety.) But transit security programs tend to focus on the vehicles themselves, neglecting open and public spaces such as bus stops and parking lots.

Transit agencies also shouldn't unwittingly feed a narrative of danger. A 2017 SFMTA safety poster, meant to caution riders not to use their phones, showed a scene from a nightmare: a darkened and empty train, where a hooded figure loomed over a woman.[14]

None of this is to doubt the fear and trauma that is regularly caused by interactions on transit. Women, in particular, are discomfited by waiting for the bus in neighborhoods that feel unsafe.[15] NYU's Rudin Center for Transportation Policy and Management has found that women are more likely than men to be harassed or feel unsafe or at risk on public transit and that women spend $25 to $50 per month more on private car travel than men to avoid perceived safety risk on transit (for example, to avoid late-night transit trips).[16]

What the Detroit bus operators who applaud more police and the OPAL activists who oppose more police have in common is that they want more of a human presence in transit and confidence that authorities will respond when called, in ways that keep riders safe. That can mean more outreach staff connecting homeless riders with services; Philadelphia's Southeastern Pennsylvania Transportation Authority (SEPTA) has even partnered with local nonprofits to open a homeless service center in one of its rail stations.[17] It might mean clearer ways to report harassment. It might mean more staff in the system who are unarmed but can provide safety in other ways.

Fair Fare Policy

More than once I've had to go to a convenience store to buy something in order to have exact change for bus fare. One morning in Charlotte I came out of the store just as the bus pulled out—a galling experience in a world where you can summon a taxi or unlock a bike using your smartphone.

Cash is a hassle for both bus operators and riders. Paying in cash tends to take longer than flashing a pass or tapping a card, delaying everyone. Accepting cash requires more complicated farebox equipment, especially if the fareboxes have to give change. On the (now relatively few) buses where operators themselves carry change, theft and robbery are a risk.

Transit operators have been trying to stop riders from using cash almost since the first omnibus plied its trade; in the United States, the transit token, the first fare payment technology, dates to 1831.[18] Today's transit agencies are upgrading fare collection systems to include smartphone ticketing apps, smartcards with accounts that can be checked and reloaded online, and "open payment" systems that will let riders use contactless bank cards or pay by tapping their phone.

All of these offer more convenience for both agencies and riders. But discussions about fare system technology often sidestep what would be more fruitful discussions about fare *policy*. New fare payment systems offer big opportunities to make the bus more efficient and equitable.

Transit fares often make arbitrary distinctions between riders, because of technological restrictions or historical inertia. One arbitrary policy that should disappear entirely from bus systems is charging riders to transfer between buses. Consider a grid of frequent bus lines, with a set of routes going north–south intersecting a set of routes traveling east–west. Why should a bus rider who has to go 2 miles in a diagonal line be charged more than someone who has to go 2 miles in a straight line?

And yet some agencies (such as Philadelphia's SEPTA) maintain transfer fees, even though even a 1990s-era magnetic stripe card is sophisticated enough to encode a free transfer. This is an anachronistic kind of extortion, as if Amazon charged you a "restocking fee" for canceling your order of an online streaming video.

Another inequitable disparity in transit is that lower-income riders often end up paying more than wealthy ones because they can only afford to pay by the ride. Most transit agencies have some type of unlimited pass. An agency where a single-ride bus fare costs $2 might sell a seven-day pass for $20, meaning anyone who takes more than ten rides a week saves money by buying the pass. But the poorest riders may have trouble saving for a $20 pass and end up paying more in single fares.

Lower-income riders often end up paying more than wealthy ones because they can only afford to pay by the ride.

Transit smartcard technology gives agencies the power to end this unfairness through "fare capping." A system with fare capping can track how many times the holder uses transit in a week and automatically "cap" the fare at the cost of the weekly pass. Once a person has spent $20 in a week on transit, any additional rides are free. (The same principle can be applied to monthly passes.)

When transit agencies don't implement new fare collection systems with an eye to equity, they can actually make things worse for many bus riders. In Chicago, the regional Ventra farecard launched with the ability to be used as a prepaid debit card, touted as a way for unbanked people to get into the banking system. But using the debit feature subjected people to predatory fees, such as a $2 charge for calling customer service and a $10/hour fee for "account research" if users disputed a charge.[19] (The debit feature was ultimately discontinued.)

Rider Costs in a System With a $2 Single-Ride Fare and $20 Seven-Day Pass

Scenario	Cost without Fare Capping	Cost with Fare Capping
Buys a 7-day pass and rides 14 times in a week	$20	$20
Pays per ride and rides 14 times in a week	$28	$20 (rider pays $2/ride for the first ten rides; her subsequent four rides are free)

SEPTA's new farecard, the SEPTA Key, began its rollout in 2016. This new fare system was the perfect time for the agency to eliminate its transfer fee. But SEPTA has not, and it has even gotten rid of the ability to buy paper transfers.[20] This means that bus riders who pay cash now have to pay a full second fare if they transfer to another bus.

Make It Easy to Pay

One of the best ways to make transit intuitive is to get people transit passes through their school, job, or apartment building. That takes a lot of the guesswork out of transit, and it makes transit seem normal and natural. In Seattle, as many as 60 percent of transit users use monthly passes from employers, partly because of supportive state policy that requires big employers to incentivize nondriving commutes.

In the Bay Area, many residential complexes provide free or discounted transit passes to tenants, thanks to local laws that allow denser zoning for buildings that incentivize alternatives to driving (the advocacy group TransForm deserves a lot of credit for lobbying for these changes).

And across the country, hundreds of colleges and universities include transit passes in the cost of students' tuition, boosting transit ridership and helping university campuses avoid building expensive parking lots.

Transit advocates are increasingly calling on cities and transit agencies to extend this same convenience to poor and young people.

Transit research generally shows that raising fares helps transit agencies' bottom line; higher fares drive some riders away (for every 10 percent increase in transit fares, expect a ridership drop of 2 to 5 percent), but not that many, so fare increases are revenue positive for agencies.[21]

But as Baruch University's Alex Perotta has found, transit fares can be an enormous hardship for poor riders.[22] Perotta talked with low-income New Yorkers to complete her dissertation. Many told her that they skimped on groceries, paid rent late, or delayed adding minutes to their cell phones. Others would try to evade the fare when possible.

When transit agencies don't implement new fare collection systems with an eye to equity, they can actually make things worse for many bus riders.

"Fair fares" programs that offer reduced fares for low-income people help bridge the gulf in places such as Seattle and New York, where transit is used by many middle- and high-earning riders who can absorb price increases.

Seattle's ORCA Lift program offers half-priced fares for riders with household income that is less than twice the federal poverty line. King County officials got widespread enrollment by relying on a network of health clinics, community centers, and nonprofits that had helped sign up residents for health insurance under the Affordable Care Act.[23]

In New York City, the membership organization Riders Alliance joined forces with the poverty think tank Community Service Society and others to win a low-income fare program that began in 2019, although only a small number of people were initially able to take advantage of it because of an underwhelming rollout by city government.[24]

TriMet introduced a low-income fare program in 2018. Not surprisingly, the advocates at OPAL were in the mix. According to OPAL's Lopez, the fare program was their top priority as voted on

Figures 5.1a (left) and 5.1b (right)   The Youth Environmental Justice Alliance's "YouthPass to the Future" combined survey data with testimonials from individual students about how youth transit passes helped them succeed in school, work, and volunteering. (Image courtesy OPAL.)

by their members. But that wasn't the only pass program the group was working on. Since 2009, students in Portland Public Schools have received free transit passes during the school year. But these were not extended to students in two other school districts within the city of Portland's borders, Parkrose and David Douglas.

OPAL's youth pass campaign was run by student members of an OPAL program called the Youth Environmental Justice Alliance. Their members talked to their fellow students at three schools, publishing a "YouthPass to the Future" report that used survey research to call for change.[25] At David Douglas High School, where more than 75 percent of students qualify for free or reduced-price lunch, OPAL found that half of students used TriMet to get to school. Another four in ten students said that they had missed class because they had missed the school bus; a youth transit pass could allow them to take the public bus as an alternative.

Youth organizers complemented this hard data with earnest stories, profiling students who stayed at school until 9 p.m. so their family could pick them up from activities, walked home for lack of bus fare, and used TriMet to run errands for their parents. According to Fleek, the report was enormously influential, winning an expansion of YouthPass with funding from TriMet, the school districts, and the city of Portland that has lasted for 2 years.

"There's a two-pronged approach to all the campaigns that we run, and it's basically the 'head game' and the 'heart game,'" Fleek said. "There are some decisionmakers who will not listen to you unless you've got hard data, and there are some who will only listen to you if you've got a sob story. But we have to have both."

Youth transit passes help young people live fuller lives. They may also help seed a new generation of transit riders. Researchers Michael Smart and Nicholas Klein have found that there is an exposure effect when it comes to the bus; riding transit at any age makes people more likely to ride it later.[26]

Fare Evasion

Fare evasion—when someone gets on the bus and doesn't pay—is a routine enough occurrence that buses typically have a fare evasion key. This button gets pressed by the operator when someone boards without a fare, so that the transit agency can accurately count ridership figures and identify places where many riders skip the fare.

Youth transit passes help young people live fuller lives. They may also help seed a new generation of transit riders.

Of course, transit agencies want to maximize their revenue. But they should resist the urge to get caught up in moralistic dudgeon. A 2017 Portland television spot warned that "thousands of bus riders don't pay, and most get away with it."[27] Charles Moerdler, a board member at New York's Metropolitan Transportation Authority until 2019, has called riders who don't pay "thieves" and "lawbreakers."[28] (Moerdler is perhaps the last person who should make this argument, as he has been repeatedly caught by the media breaking parking laws with his MTA-issued placard.)

On closer inspection, bus fare evasion often turns out to be a crime of poverty or a sign of the system's inconvenience.

Researchers who have studied the issue have found that a small number of people are hardcore fare evaders who almost never pay (a small group is responsible for a lot of farebeating, in other words).[29] But a much larger number of people fall into the category of "'not my fault' evaders," who have been stymied by something in the transit system itself. This category includes people who jump on an arriving train because the line at the ticket machine is too long or someone who can't figure out how to use the ticket machine in the first place. These people might literally be at fault, but they wouldn't have skipped the fare if paying it was easy.

And buses, in particular, can be a pain to pay for. The consequences of missing an infrequent bus are high, meaning that someone who cannot easily pay the fare is more likely to try to push on. Buses often require people paying in cash to use exact change; do you routinely carry $2.75 in quarters?

And unlike train stations, most bus stops lack machines where you can buy a pass. Ideally, transit agencies have partnerships with pharmacies, groceries, and other stores to make transit fare media widely available for purchase. But often, these retail networks are sparse and poorly advertised. This raises the specter of people being thrown into the criminal justice system because they didn't realize they were down to the last 75 cents on their farecard, because they couldn't break a $20 bill, or because they didn't want to go a mile out of their way to find a store selling a transit pass.

The research that exists on the demographics of fare evaders suggests that evasion is often the result of economic desperation. A team of researchers from Virginia Tech and NYU found that in the District of Columbia, every area with a high rate of bus fare evasion also had a high rate of poverty. They also found that the three census block groups with the highest rates of fare evasion did not have a single machine or retail store where someone could buy or reload money on the SmarTrip fare card.[30]

As a result, many cities are decriminalizing or otherwise changing fare evasion policy. The Washington, DC City Council made fare evasion a civil offense in 2019, eliminating the possibility of jail time for an offense.[31] California has decriminalized fare evasion by minors.[32]

In Portland, OPAL and its allies won legislative and policy changes that replaced the penalty for fare evasion, which had been a $175 fine that required a court appearance, with three less punitive options: a $75 fine for a first offense, community service, or, for poor riders, signing up for TriMet's low-income fare program.[33]

An equitable approach to fare enforcement becomes even more important as transit agencies implement all-door boarding. Letting riders board the bus at all doors is one of the most important ways to speed up the bus, but because it usually involves a proof-of-payment fare system, it adds roving fare inspectors to the system. It is critical that these personnel conduct inspections in an unbiased way and especially that fare enforcement not be conducted by armed police.

Bus fare evasion often turns out to be a crime of poverty or a sign of the system's inconvenience.

In fact, a judge in Cleveland ruled that allowing police to conduct random fare inspections on the city's Health Line bus rapid transit violates the constitutional prohibition against unreasonable search and seizure.[34] Unfortunately, the response from the Greater Cleveland Regional Transit Authority was not to use civilian staff but to abandon the idea of off-board fare collection entirely. Cleveland's Health Line has slowed down and lost riders—an inequitable result for sure.

Transit Equity Starts at Home

It is an unfair reality that transit agencies bear the burden of upstream societal failure. Underfunded shelters and overheated housing markets mean that transit agencies are asked to address homelessness. Racist criminal justice systems complicate efforts to reduce fare evasion and keep riders safe. These can feel distant from the transit professional's expertise of planning better bus routes and managing headways, yet they affect riders' experience all the same.

This means transit leaders must face them head on, in all their complexity. If there is one generalizable rule that can be applied here, it is to avoid blanket assumptions. Don't assume that riders want more police, or that they categorically reject them, without understanding the local history of policing and how riders have experienced it. Don't assume that new fare systems will be an improvement for everyone. Listening to and learning from riders' experiences is the best way forward.

Discussions of safety and security, fare policy, and service planning go to the heart of a transit agency's and a community's values.

Therefore, they're a natural focus for transit agency boards, and it's especially important that those boards reflect the people who ride transit.

Transit advocacy groups also need to work with, understand the perspectives of, and listen to the voices of marginalized communities. There are many transit best practices that American agencies should import from other places, from all-door boarding to smarter fare payment systems. But advocates need to recognize how these can collide with some of America's worst practices, such as violent policing and a patchy welfare system.

By itself, better bus service cannot fully remedy the many structural harms imposed on marginalized groups. But agencies can intentionally plan their service in ways that aim to further equitable access to our cities. All bus riders deserve a transit experience that is safe, welcoming, and intuitive. That may never be completely possible in an oppressive and flawed world. But planners can work for transit that improves access and strive to avoid inflicting greater harm.

06 GERRYMANDERING THE BUS

—

Journalist Henry Grabar has called the bus network in the Detroit region "America's worst transit system."[1] Metro Detroit is home to one of the highest shares of carless households in the country, and those residents have one of the longest average commutes to work and school, at 10.4 miles. Three of every five Detroit residents work in the suburbs, and three-quarters of people who work in Detroit commute in from outside the city.

Despite this, regional transit is abysmal. Buses stop every few blocks, prolonging the journey for riders. Suburban towns are allowed to opt out of paying for bus service, and most buses stop at the Detroit city line, forcing riders to transfer between city and suburban buses.

In 2018, Wayne County executive Warren Evans released a video putting himself in the shoes of a Detroit bus rider trying to get to work at a Best Buy in Novi. Novi is 29 miles and a half-hour by car from downtown Detroit. For Evans, it took much longer: a two-and-a-half-hour trip that involved switching buses and walking for 2 miles along the unpaved edge of a highway. Novi is an "opt-out community" without bus service.

This shrinks Novi's labor pool as well. According to the Center for Neighborhood Technology's AllTransit tool, transit allows only 1,450 potential workers to access Novi jobs within a half-hour. In the neighboring city of Farmington Hills, which is served by the SMART system, bus service gives employers access to 22,427 potential workers.

The Detroit metro region spends just $69 per capita on public transit, a third of what Cleveland does and a ninth of what Seattle does. Several efforts to raise taxes to pay for improvements have been rejected by suburban voters or blocked by suburban leaders.

The deliberate failure of the region's leaders to properly plan or fund transit should be seen as an example of "mobility redlining."

It's one of many ways that exclusionary regional and state politics can distort the governance of transit and make improving it more difficult. Fixing the bus in these places often requires central cities to put transit at the top of their agendas and strong coalitions that can overcome overt hostility to bus riders.

Regional Exclusion

Toxic relationships between cities and their suburbs are often rooted in racism. I'm not mincing my words, and neither has L. Brooks Patterson, the longtime leader of Oakland County, one of the fiercest opponents of regional transit in southeast Michigan. When asked by a *New Yorker* reporter in 2014 how Detroit could fix its finances, Patterson joked, "What we're gonna do is turn Detroit into an Indian reservation, where we herd all the Indians into the city, build a fence around it, and then throw in the blankets and corn."[2]

The deliberate failure of the region's leaders
to properly plan or fund transit should be seen
as an example of "mobility redlining."

These political dynamics often play out within metropolitan planning organizations (MPOs), which decide how to distribute some types of federal transportation funds and often overrepresent the suburbs. At the MPO that represents greater Cleveland, for example, the city gets to appoint six of the agency's forty members—one vote for every 64,200 residents. Rural Geauga County has three votes, one for every 31,300 of its residents.[3]

State legislatures and departments of transportation, which have control over most transportation funds, can be even more biased against urban projects, because they have little obligation to spend their funding in ways that reflect how their state's population is distributed. State legislatures even directly meddle in municipalities' ability to raise taxes for transit or build certain kinds of transit. In 2014, as Nashville was considering construction of a rapid bus project, Tennessee state legislators proposed banning bus lanes on state roads; the legislature ultimately held off on an outright ban but passed a law giving itself veto power over such projects.[4]

It is even true of transit agencies themselves. Suburban-dominated transit boards often make investment decisions that prioritize little-used rail to the edges of the region rather than well-sited and frequent services.

Many cities are learning that they will not get the frequent bus service they need through regional or state politics and are finding ways to go it alone. Places such as Salt Lake City and Denver are contemplating following Seattle's lead and buying extra bus service from regional transit agencies. Others, especially in conservative states, find themselves traversing a legislative obstacle course. A successful transit campaign in Indianapolis shows how much effort and skill is needed to make it through.

Indianapolis Breaks the Mold

Like many other Midwestern regions, Indianapolis sprawled outward throughout the latter half of the 20th century, and its expansive transit system was gradually cut back during the same time period. By the 2000s, buses were failing most city residents, including the one in five Indianapolis residents who lived in poverty.[5] In 2014, only a quarter of jobs in Indianapolis could be reached on IndyGo's frequent transit network, and only 16 percent of low-income households had access to frequent transit.

What turned it around was years of effort from an odd-bedfellows coalition of businesses and faith-based poverty advocates, as well as an idiosyncratic right-wing mayor.

In 2008, Indianapolis elected a new mayor, Greg Ballard, a conservative whom Mark Fisher, the chief policy officer at the Indy Chamber, described as part of the "first wave of the Tea Party" but who held heterodox views on energy and transportation. A retired Marine and veteran of the Gulf Wars, Ballard strongly believed that the country was too dependent on foreign oil and that it needed to support alternatives to the automobile.

The Indy Chamber, the city's leading business group, was also an enthusiastic supporter of transit as a way to attract a talented workforce and advocated a plan to build rail between the airport and downtown. But Ballard warned the group that he wouldn't support a single line that didn't improve regional mobility.

Fisher recollected that Mayor Ballard told him, "I can sell a system, but I can't sell a line, and that's all you're giving me."

Instead, the mayor asked the Indy Chamber, other business organizations and universities, and the Central Indiana Community Foundation to come up with a transportation plan for the region. They commissioned an analysis that found that transit projects would have the highest return on investment, and they recommended an expansive plan: a nine-county regional transit district that would pay for commuter rail, light rail, and expanded bus service.

This behemoth funding proposal made little headway in the state legislature, failing in 2012 and 2013 despite the support of Ballard and the business leaders.

Many cities are learning that they will not get the frequent bus service they need through regional or state politics and are finding ways to go it alone.

By this point, the pro-transit forces in Indianapolis had broadened to include the Indianapolis Congregation Action Network, a coalition of faith-based groups representing seventeen different denominations (it has since changed its name to Faith in Indiana).[6] They made an unusual pair. While the Indy Chamber focused on Republican legislators, IndyCAN talked social justice and held weekly vigils at the statehouse.[7] Whereas the Chamber talked about attracting Millennials, IndyCAN sent discussion questions to Catholic congregations asking members to reflect on how Jesus's parable of the loaves and fishes related to mass transit.[8]

In 2014, the advocates finally broke through, securing passage of legislation authorizing local transit funding increases. State legislators, however, had managed to insert a ban on light rail into the law. And the nine-county district was a no-go. Instead, the state agreed to grant individual counties the ability to raise their own taxes to pay for transit, if voters first approved it in a nonbinding referendum.[9]

Advocates had won at the state legislature after years of work—and had years to go.

Now that new transit revenue was a potential reality, the county transit agency, IndyGo, had a responsibility to show citizens what it might do with it. And it had hired Jarrett Walker + Associates, the consultancy that worked on the Houston and Columbus network redesigns, to lead an analysis of its bus network.

The resulting plan included three rapid bus corridors and a redrawn local bus network that put more focus on frequent buses in high-ridership areas. Service would increase by 70 percent, opening up frequent transit access to half of jobs and half of low-income households in the county.

Knowing that the decision to put the transit plan on the ballot could occur later that year, IndyGo and the region's metropolitan planning organization ran a blitz of public outreach sessions to educate residents on how the bus network would expand if the county were to raise revenue for transit. Agency staff organized or attended twenty-five meetings over the course of 10 weeks in February, March, and April. These included open houses at neighborhood libraries and affordable housing complexes, neighborhood association meetings, young-professional dinners, and even a downtown salon called "tech + fashion + transit + urban."[10]

Although these sessions were nonpolitical, the agencies could present statistics that showed how far behind on the transit scoreboard Indianapolis was. Although it was the 33rd largest region in America, Indianapolis was 86th in transit investment per capita. But an expanded bus network could give a majority of low-income households access to frequent transit.[11]

IndyGo also had a secret weapon: Fisher, who had been named to the agency's board in late 2014. Whereas IndyGo staff were restricted to giving neutral presentations, Fisher was often present to follow up and offer his personal opinion as a board member—which was that expanded bus service made sense.

Once the City–County Council voted in May 2016 to put the measure on the November ballot, campaign efforts sprang into action.

The Indy Chamber assembled a "grasstops" coalition, Transit Drives Indy, that represented many of the region's growth-focused leaders, including MIBOR, the regional realtors' association; Indy-Hub, a young professionals' organization; the state AARP chapter; the Indiana Urban League; and the Indiana Latino Institute.

Together, they raised $500,000 to fund polling and voter modeling, direct mail, social media advertising, and other voter engagement efforts.

Their polling found that accessibility resonated with Marion County voters. "From our earliest poll to our last poll, the message that resonated across demographic groups was, 'Transit is an investment in providing better access to jobs, education and health care,'" Fisher said. Some form of that message made its way into mailers, TV spots, and social media.

Meanwhile, IndyCAN headed a grassroots mobilization effort. While the organization sat alongside business leaders and realtors on the steering committee of Transit Drives Indy, its real strength was in pews and living rooms. IndyCAN's four full-time staff and two paid fellows organized volunteers to knock on people's doors, make calls, text, and host community events and house parties.

The key outcome of those activities, in many cases, was voter turnout. As Nicole Barnes, IndyCAN's director of voter engagement, explained, the fact that the referendum was nonbinding meant that the win had to be large enough to demonstrate a popular mandate. The transit referendum was also part of a broader project of building power among people of color and low-income voters. IndyCAN's "voter universe"—the pool of potential voters that organizers wanted to turn out—was 82 percent African American. More than half were "low-propensity" voters who did not have a history of voting.[12]

The polling that the Indy Chamber and MIBOR paid for helped IndyCAN's door-to-door messaging. Barnes said that, depending on whether the person who answered the door had liberal or conservative tendencies, IndyCAN volunteers could steer the conversation in one of two directions by asking "Is Indianapolis a fair city?" or "Is Indianapolis a competitive city?" Regardless of how the conversation started, the volunteers tried to steer it to the same place: "The people who need the jobs the most can't even access the jobs," Barnes said.

IndyCAN also linked lack of transit access to broader structures that hurt residents of color. "We had to engage people on a variety of levels. . . . Folks who may not necessarily use the bus system, they were able to see the connection to mass incarceration and how it all works together," Barnes said. "We can't have people locked up at the rates that they are, and we also can't suffocate communities of color—who utilize the bus the most."

On Election Day, IndyCAN had teams of poll watchers across the city. At one polling station, where lines ran around the block and rain was coming down, Barnes recalled, "We ran to CVS, we bought ponchos; we went to Speedway, got people hot chocolate and umbrellas. Just to make sure that people stood in line and stayed there to vote. We needed them to understand . . . even the way the voting system is set up is a way to keep us from getting what we need, so we need you to push through."

The message that resonated across demographic groups was, "Transit is an investment in providing better access to jobs, education and health care."

After the last ballot was counted, six in ten Marion County voters had said yes to more transit. IndyCAN's organizers had signed up more than 1,200 volunteers, who had collectively made more than 165,000 phone calls. Pro-transit television ads had been seen 1.7 million times.[13] According to Fisher, it was the first time a referendum on raising taxes for a service other than education had passed in Indiana history. The popular mandate proved to be convincing enough for Indianapolis's City–County Council, which approved the income tax increase a few months later by another lopsided vote, 17–8.

Since then, IndyGo has been gradually ramping up to the promised increase in bus service. The agency made a first set of service expansions in 2018, and transit ridership increased by 3 percent, turning around years of decline. The Red Line is set to open by 2020, providing a spine of high-quality bus service connecting key destinations.

"We took our time, we got a system that made sense, and we very clearly communicated what people were going to get in return for their investment," Fisher said. "We [didn't start] off with . . . a line to the most affluent suburb, or the airport. [It was], 'how are we going to design a system that the taxpayers—the people that live in this community—are going to be able to take advantage of?'"

Transit *101* in Dallas

Dallas Area Rapid Transit (DART) is known for having the longest light rail system in the United States. But it hardly offers much value to its riders. A damning analysis from the University of Texas at Arlington revealed, in the words of *D Magazine*, "DART's system-wide inadequacy."[14]

Only 20 percent of Dallas residents have access to high-frequency service during the morning and afternoon peak hours, and in the middle of the day, just 9 percent do. Transit planning in Dallas has failed low-income people. More than 73 percent of Section 8 multi-family affordable housing developments in Dallas are unaffordable when the cost of transportation is factored in.

At its core, the problem with DART is that, for most of its history, its leaders have focused on building rail to as many places as possible. DART's board gives the city of Dallas a slight majority, with eight members representing the city and seven appointed by suburban municipalities. But decisions on the agency's finances, service plan, and capital projects require a two-thirds vote, giving the suburbs veto power.[15]

"It's created basically a system where to keep everybody happy, [Dallas] gets a project, then the suburbs get a project," said Patrick Kennedy, a board member from the city of Dallas. This has short-changed bus riders: "Most of our riders are on the south side; . . . bus service improvements essentially get labeled a 'Dallas thing.'"

Kennedy was named to DART's board after Dallas mayor Mike Rawlings and the City Council had finally had enough of DART's light rail regionalism. After five DART board members who represented the city voted to advance the Cotton Belt light rail line, the latest in a series of suburban rail projects, the council kicked them off the board.

Kennedy, an urban planner who had been advocating for transit-oriented land use and walkability for several years, was one of a new cohort of city board members focused on Dallas's needs instead of regional comity.

He quickly started looking into old analyses of DART's bus service, which made it clear how inadequately bus riders were being treated. "Seventy-plus percent of the routes had their highest ridership midday, but the lowest frequency," he said. "Before we can even talk about attracting new riders and increased ridership, we've got to improve the lives of our existing riders. We've got 60-minute midday [frequencies] and many of our riders are not working 9-to-5 jobs, they're trying to get to healthcare or grocery stores because most of [south Dallas] is also a food desert."

Part of the problem on the board was a simple, technological view of rail as good transit. "Everybody had a different definition of good transit," Kennedy said. "The only way that a lot of people were defining it was by miles of light-rail tracks and whether you had a stop or not. Building light rail tracks to everybody—that's impossible, and frankly, trying to do so and spending so much on capital and debt is what hinders our operational dollars."

"Before we can even talk about attracting new riders and increased ridership, we've got to improve the lives of our existing riders."

Although Kennedy has been willing to vote against suburban projects, he has also worked, less confrontationally, to raise the level of transit understanding on the board with the aim of raising the bar for bus service. This project has come through overhauling the agency's "service standards," which outline the kinds of service DART provides and explains where different types of service are appropriate.

Before Kennedy arrived, the standards had defined only a basic, baseline expectation: Any city in DART's service area was guaranteed transit service that arrived at least once an hour. Kennedy wanted to go further, identifying places that could justify frequent service.

"[The old standards were] really just setting the floor," Kennedy said. "I wanted to create more of a hierarchy and explain the conditions that make areas appropriate for better service. Instead of just a floor, we've also set the penthouse."

Kennedy organized a series of briefings for the board, on topics such as bus network structure, frequency, and span of service. And although DART's board has not agreed to a full bus network redesign, the service standards set up more gradual reforms.

The new standards define a "core frequent network" of bus routes that run every 15 minutes at peak and 20 minutes midday.[16] They also say that if a low-performing bus route gets its service cut or removed, the operating dollars have to be reinvested in the core frequent network. In this way, service will be continually redistributed to the routes with the highest potential for ridership.

Kennedy claims that DART staff have told him this is their favorite board to work with in recent memory. "That's because our politics are no longer at odds with delivering good transit," he said.

Cities Must Lead, Right Up to Their Limits

Indianapolis's pro-transit coalition was broad, which is perhaps one reason it has broken through where other transit campaigns have not. The failed 2018 campaign in Nashville, for example, was faulted for being run primarily by business interests and failing to sufficiently engage black neighborhoods and black leaders.[17]

Reformers in Indianapolis and Dallas have made meaningful gains and sparked intelligent discussion of transit. But there are limits to what they accomplished, of course.

Indianapolis was able to dramatically increase funding for transit. But even so, the city still doesn't have a level of transit service commensurate to its population. In Dallas, Kennedy and his fellow board members were not able to defeat the Cotton Belt Line. Unlike in Houston, where a single board member could spark dramatic change because the broader politics were aligned, Kennedy's changes have been more incremental.

But by challenging the regional status quo, reformers in both cities made meaningful improvements in transit and empowered citizens for possible future success. Indiana's state legislature undid its ban of light rail. And the Analyst Institute found that IndyCAN's voter engagement strategy in the run-up to the election led to a lasting increase in civic participation afterward.[18]

07 TECHNOLOGY WON'T KILL THE BUS—UNLESS WE LET IT

—

When voters are asked to tax themselves to increase funding for public transit, most of the time the answer is yes. According to statistics compiled by the Center for Transportation Excellence (CFTE), transit referenda generally pass seven out of every ten times. But this number is inflated by a large number of routine transit tax renewal votes in places such as Perry, Michigan. When the vote is for high-profile, high-dollar, high-stakes transit investments, success is less assured. In 2018, one of the highest-profile, highest-stakes campaigns took place in Nashville.

Nashville mayor Megan Barry, the Nashville Chamber of Commerce, and a coalition of transportation advocates put their political capital behind a $5.4-billion transit plan. On May 1, Nashvillians would vote on whether they wanted to pay higher sales, hotel, business excise, and car rental taxes in order to make an investment in 26 miles of light rail, multiple rapid bus corridors, more frequent bus service, and free fares for low-income riders. Most of Nashville's Metropolitan Council members supported the plan, and early polling showed it was slightly ahead, but campaigning was vigorous on both sides.

One day before early voting began, an opponent of the plan, Metropolitan Council member Robert Swope, announced that he had an alternative transit proposal that was a better fit for Nashville's future. It was dubbed "Intelligent Transit for the IT City Nashville," and it was unveiled at an event at downtown Nashville's Wildhorse Saloon, the largest restaurant in the state.

Joined on stage by two state senators, and with other Metro Council members who opposed the transit plan in the audience, Swope described a different vision: self-driving, self-charging electric buses, along with "double-stacking" the interstate highways around the city. His plan, he argued, could be completed without raising taxes and could be done more quickly than the proposed transit plan.

Like a real transportation plan, the "Intelligent Transit" plan came with financial numbers; according to a press release, it would be financed with "$400 million in private dollars, $150 million from the state," $700 million in federal funds, and $400 million from surrounding counties. It also name-dropped real partners. Not only would the proposal "be implemented with the assistance of the State of Tennessee within the next three years," its autonomous buses would be charged at stations "created by the Oak Ridge National Laboratories and developed by Qualcomm."

But like the false airfields built by Britain's Royal Air Ministry to fool German bombers during World War II, the Swope proposal only looked like a real transportation plan from a distance. Even the slightest scrutiny revealed it to be the equivalent of a movie set. Quizzical analysts told the *Tennessean* that double-stacked highways would be extremely expensive and complicated.[1] Staff from the Tennessee Department of Transportation said they had not been involved in the plan. No one from Oak Ridge or Qualcomm appeared on stage.

None of that mattered, because the point was not to produce a meaningful alternative to the Nashville transit plan. It was to seed the idea in voters' minds that future technologies made transit obsolete.

The Nashville transit campaign ended in humiliation for supporters, losing at the ballot box by a nearly two-to-one margin. Opponents skillfully organized opposition to the plan in African American neighborhoods, and the campaign's most popular champion, Mayor Barry, had to resign her office 2 months before the vote because of a personal scandal.[2] These factors were probably far more decisive than talk of driverless cars on stacked highways.

But the Swope plan made a difference on the margins. The launch event was covered by Nashville's main newspaper, business journal, public radio station, and alternative media. The pro-transit campaign spent time and energy debunking the plan, rushing out "mythbusting" documents when it could have spent more time organizing get-out-the-vote efforts.

Across the country, Swope's counterparts are claiming that technologies such as autonomous vehicles, microtransit, and Uber and Lyft will inevitably replace trains and buses. The evidence suggests that will happen only if cities buy the snake oil.

Distraction and Hype

Those who are closest to autonomous vehicle technology say it will be a long time, if ever, before fully autonomous vehicles can coexist on streets with pedestrians and human drivers.

It will be a long time, if ever, before fully autonomous vehicles can coexist on streets with pedestrians and human drivers.

In a 2017 blog post, the CEO of Argo AI, which has received $1 billion from Ford to work on self-driving technology, wrote that "those who think self-driving cars will be ubiquitous on city streets . . . in a few years are not well connected to the state of the art or committed to the safe deployment of the technology."[3] That same year, a prominent investor in autonomous vehicle startups concluded that "autonomous technology is currently where computing was in the 60s."[4]

Waymo, a subsidiary of Alphabet, Google's parent company, is considered (along with General Motors) one of the leaders in the autonomous vehicle industry. But at a November 2018 conference, Waymo CEO John Krafcik told attendees that "autonomy will always have some constraints" and that he doubted the technology would ever be capable of driving at all times of year, in all kinds of weather.[5]

That is not the message that anti-transit ideologues are pushing. In Nashville, Swope warned audience members to think carefully about whether they wanted to vote for the "1850s technology" of buses and trains, promising that the self-driving transit of his plan would "be implemented within the next 12 months, not 12 years."

Mark Fisher, the executive who led the Indy Chamber's transit campaign, told me that throughout the 2010s, as advocates lobbied the Indiana legislature to grant cities the ability to tax themselves for transit, many legislators argued that "'we don't need transit because autonomous vehicles are going to be ubiquitous [within] the next three or four years.' . . . It was way more widespread than I would've guessed."

Microtransit, Uber and Lyft, and autonomous vehicles cater perfectly to the futurist instinct. They are cloaked in Silicon Valley mystique, often with big-talking founders and attention paid to branding. The launch event for Swope's "Intelligent Transit" plan included the CEO of a "smart cities" company, who appeared via teleconference because he was on a business trip in Tokyo, where he had met with the Japanese prime minister. The press release for the plan announced that it included "the world's first carbon-positive electric vehicles (EV) and autonomous vehicles (AV) for mass transportation on a global basis."[6]

Although this tactic looks to the future, it is quite old. For decades, it has been a common tactic of conservative think tanks to fight against plans for high-capacity transit by pointing cities to some other technology instead, such as dynamically priced high-occupancy toll lanes, bus rapid transit (as an argument against proposed rail projects), and personal rapid transit. Driverless cars and data-driven vans are just the newest technology filling in the blank.

It has been a common tactic of conservative think tanks to fight against plans for high-capacity transit by pointing cities to some other technology instead.

For many years, Cato Institute senior fellow Randal O'Toole opposed plans for rail by calling on cities to make bus improvements instead. But a July 2018 post on his Cato Institute blog gives away the game. In it, he wrote that "in the short run, agencies can experiment with low-cost improvements in bus service," but ultimately they "need to back out of transit services that fewer and fewer people are using . . . [and] die with dignity."[7]

Had the Nashville "Intelligent Transit" plan been released in good faith, you would have expected its backers to keep pushing it after the May election. After all, the city still faces major transportation challenges. But while writing this book, I saw that the "Intelligent Transit" website had not been updated since Swope's press conference on April 10, 2018. The only action one could take on its "Get Involved" page was to sign a petition against the transit plan that was actually put before voters. Technology won't kill transit, but it can be a handy alibi for those who want to stick in the knife.

Some decisionmakers may still wonder: Is it worth making public transit better if some new technology could come along to supplant it?

When it comes to buses, one obvious response is that improved bus service can be achieved in months and years. Predicting technological progress is like trying to time the stock market; why not make a sure investment in improving citizens' lives today?

A more fundamental answer, as I wrote earlier, is that the basic geometry of cities makes high-capacity train and bus service essential. There is a reason that the American cities most closely associated with the tech industry—San Francisco and Seattle—have made relentless improvements to bus service and seen bus ridership increases as a result. (And that's not even taking into account the vast fleets of private buses that take many Silicon Valley workers to their corporate campuses every morning.)

Remembering the geometric rules that govern transit will also help decisionmakers think about another trend that is sweeping the country: microtransit.

Microtransit: Innovation for the Transit Fringe

Dozens of transit agencies have experimented with microtransit. Generally speaking, microtransit uses small vehicles (such as vans or minibuses) and allows riders to schedule pickups in advance or in real time, often within a defined zone.

Los Angeles Metro's microtransit page asks potential riders to "Imagine a transit experience in which you can be picked up and dropped off where you want when you want," promising a "new service [that] is flexible and convenient for customers no matter where you're heading." It sounds, in fact, like a publicly operated TNC (and news clips sometimes describe microtransit as "Uber for buses").

But this kind of service isn't actually new. It's an evolution of an older technology, the dial-a-ride service. Many transit agencies have long run dial-a-ride service in areas with little demand, allowing customers to book rides in advance in a defined area. What microtransit brings to the table is the power of the smartphone reservation and a promise of service on demand, not scheduled hours ahead.

Like TNCs, microtransit appears to be a mode that can satisfy customers, but it has limited ability to scale.

AC Transit, the operator in Oakland and the eastern part of the Bay Area, tried replacing a low-performing fixed-route bus with a "Flex" microtransit service in 2016. The service used wheelchair-accessible vehicles, allowed customers without smartphones or bank accounts to book and pay for trips, and had translation available for every step of the process. It used the agency's unionized operators and had the same fare as regular bus service. It was cost-neutral, using the same service hours that had been assigned to the fixed-route bus.

The people who did use AC Transit's Flex service said they preferred it to regular bus service. But AC Transit project manager John Urgo concluded, "There's no getting around the fact that [the on-demand pilot carried] fewer passengers per hour than even a low ridership fixed route."[8]

Jarrett Walker outlined the fundamental challenge to on-demand transportation in an article for *The Atlantic*:

> Visualize a low-density suburb, with requests scattered over a wide area. How many people's doors can a driver get to in an hour, including the minute or two that the customer spends grabbing their things and boarding? The intuitively obvious answer is the right one: not very many.[9]

Ultimately, AC Transit's Flex pilot handled three rides per hour, less than half the productivity of the bus it replaced. At peak, it handled seven rides per hour. A typical low-performing bus might handle twelve.

Microtransit might offer an incremental improvement in providing coverage transit service. That's how Seattle's King County Metro frames these services in its Community Connections Program. It describes on-demand microtransit, traditional dial-a-ride, and flexible shuttles (which have prescribed routes but can deviate on request) as solutions "for areas of King County that don't have the infrastructure, density, or land use to support regular, fixed-route bus service." It's not an open-ended experiment but has a defined budget and metrics created in consultation with municipalities.

But the majority of cities need to devote most of their energy to making high-capacity, fixed-route transit perform better in the places where it can. When existing bus routes are unreliable and slow, focusing attention on microtransit is like trying to perfect dessert at a restaurant that routinely burns the entrees. If effectively serving the most riders is the key goal, then the question of how to replace the bus on the urban fringe is less important than the need to make the bus work in busy corridors.

A Real-Time Revolution for Buses

One arena in which private mobility companies tend to have a leg up on the bus is customer information. Calling a car through Uber takes a few taps of a finger. Using a bus can involve navigating inaccurate schedule information, using websites that don't have bus maps, and looking for a bus stop that doesn't even have the route number on it.

> The question of how to replace the bus on the urban fringe is less important than the need to make the bus work in busy corridors.

Candace Brakewood at the University of Tennessee and Kari Watkins of Georgia Tech have found a surprising range of benefits from better real-time information.[10] Having a "countdown clock" at your bus stop makes the wait *feel* shorter. But several studies have also found that real-time information can actually reduce people's transit trip times.

That's largely because of two things: When people check real-time information on their phone, they can delay their trip to the bus stop (and, say, buy a snack) if they see the bus is running late. More profoundly, in complex transit networks where people have multiple options for completing their trip, accurate information allows people to make informed choices. Someone who normally takes a bus to a light rail station might check her phone, see that the light rail is suffering disruptions, and choose to take a different bus directly to her destination instead.

There's uncharted potential to give riders more types of information, so that these types of benefits aren't restricted to smartphone-savvy riders. The newest generation of buses in New York City has high-quality LCD displays on the bus itself, displaying where the bus is on a map, the next several stops on the route, and arrival times for connecting buses.

The technology for bus stop information, too, has gotten better every year. When the SFMTA installed some of the first real-time bus information signs in the country in 1999, they used LED signs that could only display a few words of text. Transit agencies are now using LCD signs that can display more information, in multiple languages, and "e-ink" displays (like the screen of a Kindle e-reader) that are easy to power with solar energy and easy to read in bright sun.

SFMTA's Jason Lee, who is heading the agency's "next generation" customer information effort, envisions bus stop signs and smartphone apps that can tell riders far more than when the next bus is coming.[11] Lee hopes that the agency's next system also has information about how crowded the next bus is, exactly where the bus is on the route, and whether buses will be arriving on parallel streets.

More accurate real-time information technology even helps public agencies track transit performance and plan for the future. The NYC Department of Transportation has used data from the MTA's bus-tracking system to pinpoint intersections and blocks where buses move particularly slowly, informing future street design projects to keep bus riders on the go.[12]

And it can enable better service on those buses. Remember from Chapter 3 that many frequent bus routes are run off set schedules, padded with slack time that slows riders down. Active headway management can speed up frequent routes, but more dispatchers are needed to monitor headways on the route.

Better real-time information makes it possible to start automating parts of this process. The Alameda–Contra Costa Transit District, in Oakland, tried to use headway-based management in the early 2000s but abandoned the effort because the radio-based technology of the time updated bus locations only every 2–3 minutes.[13] Now that newer on-bus transponders can "poll" a bus's location every

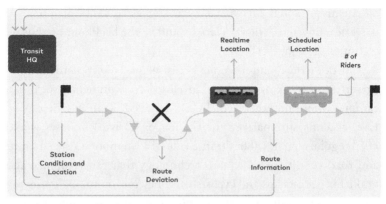

Figure 7.1   "Where can I find my bus?" is a simple question. But building an app or service that can answer it requires that the transit agency track several sources of data. (Image courtesy TransitCenter.)

30 seconds, they are taking another look. Georgia Tech researcher Simon Berrebi and others have written sophisticated software algorithms that dynamically adjust how long bus operators are asked to wait at control points, in ways that help prevent service gaps before they begin and smooth them out after.

Fully realizing the promise of data requires that transit agencies become effective stewards of data. Transit leaders need to value the collection of data and be willing to open it up for outside use. As TransitCenter and the Rocky Mountain Institute wrote in a 2019 report, at most agencies "there is no 'state of good repair' mindset around improving data infrastructure."[14] Providing more and better data requires staff dedicated to cleaning it, monitoring it, and liaising with third-party developers.

Automating Transit

Labor costs are the biggest chunk of transit operating expenses. Automation cuts that down, which is one reason many rail and monorail lines around the world are automated.

Several transit agencies are exploring the potential for automating buses as well, which would change the equation on transit viability. Bus routes that run through spread-out land uses might look more financially viable without the need for an operator. The CEO of Austin's Capital Metro has even suggested that "platoons" of driverless buses in dedicated lanes could be the backbone of a future transit expansion.[15]

But the road to autonomous buses seems as long as the road to driverless cars, except perhaps in closed environments, such as a campus where no other vehicles are allowed. Transit writer Alon Levy recently summarized the challenge: "Driverless buses would need regular updates about traffic rules (like temporary speed limits and road conditions) . . . [and] technology that can recognize and brake for pedestrians and cyclists. . . . They may not be able to avoid collisions with other drivers who do not know how to interact with driverless buses." An autonomous shuttle in Las Vegas got into a crash within 2 hours of its debut, after a truck failed to stop for it.[16]

Conversations about automation aren't meaningful without considering the number of different functions performed by the people sitting in the driver's seat.[17] Transit staff often bristle at the term *bus driver*, reflexively correcting it to *bus operator*. Driving a bus takes skill and nerve enough, yet it is just the foundation of a pyramid of tasks.

Transit staff often bristle at the term bus driver, *reflexively correcting it to* bus operator. *Driving a bus takes skill and nerve enough, yet it is just the foundation of a pyramid of tasks.*

Bus operators collect system data; for example, they often have to log when someone refuses to pay the fare or when someone loads a bicycle on the bus's front rack. They have to negotiate with riders who don't pay, which requires emotional intelligence and can lead to arguments or even assaults. They have to use judgment to attempt to stay on schedule and coordinate with dispatchers and other operators on the route to mitigate bunching. They answer questions riders have about using the transit system and relay information about delays and detours to customers. They are first responders to incidents and emergencies that take place on their bus, and they also play a role as community eyes and ears. Milwaukee bus operators have rescued nine lost or missing children off the street in recent years.[18]

It might be possible to automate some of these tasks in the future. Others are safety and customer service functions that would represent a real loss to riders if eliminated. That's why it's more likely that transit technology will focus on making operators' jobs less complex, so they can be more present and provide better customer service. It's also likely that even if most driving could be automated, agencies will want some official staff presence in a 40-, 60-, or 85-passenger bus.

What does it sound like to have an adult conversation about autonomous vehicles? Houston METRO's board of directors held one in April 2018, when agency staff and representatives of Texas Southern University came to pitch the board's Capital and Strategic Planning Committee on a test run of an autonomous shuttle.

The project they pitched would see the shuttle run back and forth on Tiger Walk, a pedestrianized part of the Texas Southern campus. This raised concerns for Christof Spieler, the board member who had championed METRO's bus network redesign 3 years earlier.

Spieler pointed out that there was little to learn from running service through a pedestrian mall. "It's a fairly limited application if we're trying to figure out what ridership would be," he said. "We're not learning anything about how the vehicle reacts in mixed traffic . . . and we're not really learning much about how this works as a first- and last-mile [connector] because it really doesn't have much in terms of transit connection."

Spieler and other committee members ultimately recommended that the full board approve the shuttle but directed staff to move as quickly as possible to expand the pilot through a nearby parking lot that connected to a light rail station, so that the agency could collect more meaningful data.

Reflecting on that meeting, Spieler told me that transit agencies need to keep goals at the front of their mind. "Every new technology is a tool, and the reason you use a tool is because you're trying to accomplish something. [If] we're showing off a new technology, you know, is it a gadget fair, or is it an actual worthwhile exercise that will help us make better transit? What can these autonomous vehicles do better than whatever we have right now? What problem are we trying to solve?"

That last question is key, not just for transit board members but for everyone working to shape transportation in their city.

Seize the Future, Don't Surrender It

Daniel Sperling and affiliated researchers at the University of California, Davis, have said that "three revolutions" in transportation can help create better places.[19] The first revolution is replacing fossil fuel vehicles with electric, to reduce emissions. The second is phasing out human driving in favor of autonomous vehicles, to improve traffic safety. The third is replacing personally owned vehicles with shared fleets, to maximize the efficiency of transportation and avoid a future where personal cars lead to an explosion of new traffic.

Of these "three revolutions," encouraging shared rides is the most dependent on government policy. It won't happen without using the right metrics to measure transportation progress. For example, if cities measure the success of a street based on how many people it moves, instead of how many vehicles, they give more space-efficient modes such as transit, biking, and pooled trips the credit they deserve.

If cities measure the success of a street based on how many people it moves, instead of how many vehicles, they give more space-efficient modes such as transit, biking, and pooled trips the credit they deserve.

It is difficult to see future cities mustering the will to properly incentivize shared rides tomorrow if they don't start by prioritizing transit, the most popular form of shared mobility that exists today.

Josh Sikich, who managed the Columbus bus network redesign, now advises cities on how to adapt to new transportation technologies at the consulting firm HDR. "Prioritizing transit in our public right-of-way will become even more important," he said. "We have a limited amount of space and we have to allocate that in the best way for the most people."

By creating policy frameworks that value moving people, cities can enable more egalitarian transit now while also laying a foundation for equitable future mobility.

08 BUILDING A TRANSIT NATION

—

"You can learn everything you need to know about the 7th Congressional District by riding the #1 bus from Cambridge to Roxbury," intones the narrator of one of my favorite political ads from the 2018 campaign cycle. She is a Boston City Council member named Ayanna Pressley, who unseated an incumbent member of Congress in a primary election and was elected to the House of Representatives.

"In a matter of blocks, you will see a stark visual contrast of life experiences, household median income—and quite literally, life expectancy drop by decades," Pressley said.[1] Her campaign website elaborated on the disparities in the district:

> When you board the number 1 bus in Cambridge, it's less than three miles to Dudley Station in Roxbury, but by the time you've made the 30-minute trip, the median household income in the neighborhoods around you have dropped by nearly $50,000 a year. As the bus rolls through Back Bay, the average person around you might expect to live until he or she is 92 years old, but when it arrives in Roxbury, the average life expectancy has fallen by as much as 30 years. A student riding the bus home to Dudley is, on average, nearly 20 percent less likely to graduate from high school in four years than a peer living just across the Charles.
>
> These types of disparities exist across the 7th District, and they are not naturally occurring; they are the legacy of decades of policies that have hardened systemic racism, increased income inequality, and advantaged the affluent.[2]

As the ad shows scenes of life from the bus's windows—a man cycling alongside, the Boston skyline, children playing basketball—Pressley describes a community-driven approach to

115

governance: "The people closest to the pain should be the closest to the power, driving and informing the policymaking."

As I watched the ad recently, I found myself wondering what Congresswoman Pressley's term will have in store for bus riders. As you've read in this book, they often are those who are furthest from the power, held out of policymaking. And although a bus route may seem the most local of concerns, many of the policies that shape that route stem from Washington.

As Pressley said, our country's spatial history—including white flight from cities, and a later, incomplete, and unequal redevelopment of urban neighborhoods—has been abetted by federal policy, including transportation. The same checkbook that paid for the Interstate Highway System, which bisected city neighborhoods and enabled the outward sprawl of suburbs, also funded transit systems from San Francisco to Atlanta, which mitigate some of that damage. But it's hardly a balanced checkbook; fights to improve urban transit ultimately cannot be divorced from efforts to right our imbalanced federal transportation policy.

Federal Transportation Policy: "Highways-as-Usual"

Although federal policy supports construction of both transit and highway infrastructure, it has a clear bias toward roads. When talking with Beltway types, you often hear about the "80–20 split"—the fact that, historically, about four out of five federal surface transportation dollars go to highway programs administered by the Federal Highway Administration, with the rest going to transit programs run by the Federal Transit Administration. Recently, this split has tipped more toward transit programs, becoming closer to a 75–25 split.

Fights to improve urban transit ultimately cannot be divorced from efforts to right our imbalanced federal transportation policy.

(A note on this and other charts that follow: I've made judgment calls about what I consider the "core programs" authorized under federal transportation law, so the exact figures and percentages shown

| "Highway" programs $39.9 billion (75.7%) | "Transit" programs $12.8 billion (24.3%) |

Figure 8.1   Core federal highway and transit programs (FY18).

in these charts may be slightly different from other breakdowns of federal transportation funding that you may have seen. At the end of the chapter, I include more information about the programs in these charts and the reasoning behind how I categorize them.)

Transit expansion also often must clear hurdles that road projects don't. Most transit expansion projects that receive federal funding get it through a program colloquially known as "New Starts" (officially the Capital Improvement Grants program). Their sponsors have to demonstrate that the project will offer mobility and congestion relief, environmental benefits, and economic development; that it is cost-effective; and that it is supported by the local land use context.

A big road widening doesn't have to show any of that. For years, the U.S. Public Interest Research Group has compiled a list of "highway boondoggles"—billions of dollars' worth of road projects that move forward when their own engineering documents show they won't solve congestion.[3]

As Christof Spieler, the former Houston METRO board member, put it on Twitter, states that want to build highways get treated like partners; transit agencies are suspect and have to prove their projects make sense.[4] The default stance is highways as usual, transit as an exception.

This spigot of road money enables further sprawl and means that even many city neighborhoods are hard to traverse except by car. It's not just that federal policy shortchanges transit; it actively creates places that transit has trouble serving.

"Our transportation [investments] end up forcing certain land use practices," said Beth Osborne, the acting assistant secretary for transportation policy during the Obama administration, who now runs the advocacy group Transportation for America. "If you design a roadway as a highway, if you design it to be wide and fast, you're not going to build a sidewalk cafe on that. There are certain things that you're not going to put there because it's not a friendly environment."

States in the Driver's Seat; Transit Taken for a Ride

National transportation policy doesn't actually shut transit out. It lets state governments do the honors.

That's because the "highway–transit split" is a porous barrier. The largest highway programs can actually pay for a wide variety of projects, including bike lanes, pedestrian crossings, and public transit. For example, the National Highway Performance Program, designed to improve interstates and major roadways, can pay for bus facilities that serve those roads and transit lines in parallel corridors.

States even have the ability to "flex" their federal funds, transferring up to half of the money they get through most federal highway programs to a transit agency in the state.[5]

This means every governor has the power to execute a radical redistribution of transportation funding. Imagine, for a moment, that you wanted to upend transportation in Ohio, which gets $1.4 billion in highway funds and less than $200 million in transit funds from the federal government. You could order Ohio's Department of Transportation (ODOT) to ship more than a half-billion of its dollars to transit agencies across the state. Furthermore, you could mandate that ODOT use its leftovers to build bus lanes on state roads, fund a statewide bus shelter program, and construct new transit centers and intersection changes to speed up buses.

In the real world, Ohio chose to flex just $33 million of its highway funds to transit and budgeted just $6.5 million in state funds for transit in 2018.[6] Meanwhile, Ohio's DOT has pursued a series of highway expansion projects, including $440 million for the "Portsmouth Bypass," $470 million to expand I-75, and $334 million to build a road called the "Opportunity Corridor."[7]

Because federal law gives states most of the money, the flexibility to use federal funds for transit is largely a tool kept under glass. In

Can be used for transit
$35.5 billion (67.4%)

Must go to transit
$12.8 billion (24.3%)

Cannot be used for transit
$4.3 billion (8.2%)

Figure 8.2   Which federal funds can be used for transit?

addition to state departments of transportation and transit agencies, a small slice of the funding is partially controlled by local governments, through MPOs, which are run by boards of local politicians. MPOs sometimes have their own inequitable politics, especially when they overrepresent suburban jurisdictions, but they are more likely to value transit, biking, and walking.

Partly that's because many state departments of transportation are staffed by engineers who view highway operations as priority number one. But, more deeply, it reflects an anti-urban politics. It's no coincidence that Ohio has one of the most gerrymandered legislatures in the country, which dilutes the power of city voters.

Funding Buses, Not Bus Operators

When it comes to buses, there's another big gap in federal transportation funding. One of the most important aspects of great bus systems is running frequent service. But almost all funding that the federal government gives to transit agencies must be used for capital expenses. Except at the smallest transit agencies, federal dollars can build and buy things but can't be used to pay bus operators to drive buses, dispatchers to monitor them, or customer service agents to tend to riders.

It wasn't always this way. Beginning in 1975, the federal government provided hundreds of millions of dollars a year in transit operating aid; by 1980, this had grown to $1.06 billion ($3.4 billion in 2019 dollars).[8] It was the Reagan administration that proposed ending this assistance; officials warned that local transit agencies had grown too dependent on federal largesse, and operating support dwindled during the George H.W. Bush and Clinton administrations. Operating aid to transit agencies in all but the smallest regions was eliminated entirely in 1998.[9]

Figure 8.3   Who chooses the projects federal transportation funds pay for?

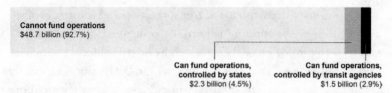

Figure 8.4   Which federal funds can support transit operations?

After the "Great Recession" of 2007–2009, this restriction led to calamity. Transit agency funding sources vary, but nearly all of them—especially local sales taxes—take a beating when the economy goes into a downturn. In 2010, the transit agency in Lorain County, Ohio laid off thirty-two of its forty-one bus operators, shrinking its bus system to just two routes running 5 days a week.[10] In St. Louis, Missouri, bus service was ended at 2,300 of 9,000 stops.[11] Across the country, almost half of transit agencies cut service; a third raised fares.[12]

The federal bias against funding transit operations held true even in the depths of the recession. The 2009 economic stimulus law provided $8.4 billion for transit, but 90 percent of it had to be used for capital projects. At the same time St. Louis transit agencies were ending service at thousands of bus stops, they were using stimulus funds to replace old rail ties. Lorain County had purchased thirteen new buses with more than $700,000 in stimulus funds, just months before laying off nearly everyone who could operate them.

These service cuts compounded the consequences of the downturn. People who had their cars repossessed saw viable transportation alternatives disappear. Americans facing a bleak job market saw their potential access to jobs shrink.

Highways-as-Usual Has Bipartisan Support

Conservatives would like to see the federal government retreat from its role in funding transit. The Heritage Foundation, for example, has recommended that the government stop spending gas tax revenue for "nonroad" uses and regularly calls on Congress to eliminate the Federal Transit Administration and phase out transit funding.[13] In 2012, a House committee passed a measure to cut all dedicated funding for federal transit programs, forcing them to rely on annual budget appropriations from Congress; the proposal ultimately collapsed after both Democrats and suburban Republican legislators refused to support it.[14] More recently, the Trump administration's proposed budgets have called for an end to the New Starts program.[15]

Democrats don't agree. In 2018, Senate Democrats released an "infrastructure blueprint" that would greatly expand programs for transit capital projects. Senate minority leader Chuck Schumer wrote in the *Washington Post* that Democrats would only pass an infrastructure bill that helps address climate change.[16]

The federal bias against funding transit operations held true even in the depths of the recession.

But the Senate Democrats' own infrastructure blueprint makes only a one-sided effort to reduce transportation emissions. That's because it would keep the existing highway programs the same, continuing to give state DOTs a free hand on road building.[17]

This is somewhat akin to an "all-of-the-above" approach to energy that embraces both renewables and continued investment in oil and gas. Environmental groups turned against such an approach several years ago. Similarly, an "all-of-the-above" approach to surface transportation doesn't cut it. It's not enough to build more transit as long as federal policy continues to subsidize the highway-and-sprawl machine.

As Osborne said, "The Republican position is to get more money in the hands of the state DOTs and let them make more decisions; the position of the Democrats has been 'spend more money in [the transportation] program.'" The result is a program that has grown in size over time but kept states in charge and continued growth in highways that cannot be justified on economic, environmental, or social grounds. That has bequeathed America the most carbon-intensive transportation system among developed countries, one that has enabled sprawl, widened economic inequality, and entrenched segregation.[18]

The current law that authorizes federal surface transportation programs, the FAST Act, is set to expire on September 30, 2020, and there's already a push to triple down on highways. In December

2018, the Transportation Research Board released a report on "future interstate needs," conducted by a committee that spanned the transportation establishment. It calls for doubling or tripling what the government currently spends just on interstate highways, to $55–$75 billion annually, to add more road miles and upgrade highways to handle autonomous and electric vehicles.[19]

It's not enough to build more transit as long as federal policy continues to subsidize the highway-and-sprawl machine.

So if one national party seeks to cut off federal support for transit, while the other is largely content with highways-as-usual, what prospects are there for a transformational rethinking of federal policy?

A Bridge to the Future

Over the last 40 years, some of the biggest changes to federal transportation policy have come through national coalitions, funded with philanthropic dollars, that have sought to bend the arc of transportation spending away from highway expansion.

In the early 1990s, the Surface Transportation Policy Project, a coalition of environmental and planning groups, played an influential role in creating the flexibility that now exists in federal highway funds, which at least gives states the option to program their funds for a variety of uses.[20]

In the late 2000s, the Transportation for America (T4A) coalition (where I worked for 2 years) worked to make federal transportation policy something more than an amorphous block grant program. T4A proposed that states should measure the progress of their transportation networks toward goals such as safety, environmental sustainability, and pavement condition.

The ambition was to move states beyond old ideas of highway performance, which focused on eliminating congestion, and recognize that it can make more sense to build in ways so that people don't have to drive as far or as much. Measuring changes in access to jobs and destinations, for example, would better capture the benefit of replacing a cul-de-sac with a connected road network that enables shorter trips or improving bus service through a network redesign.

"When you only measure traffic congestion, the only thing you can do is make traffic go faster," Osborne said. "The irony is, you can make traffic go faster and not connect people with the things they need any better than you did before."

T4A was successful in getting performance measurement requirements in the 2012 federal transportation law (Moving Ahead for Progress in the 21st Century, or MAP-21). But the legislation attached few strings to the measures. States were allowed to set their own goals, and there are no penalties for failing to make progress. The performance-based provisions of federal transportation law have been, so far, a bridge to nowhere.

As I write this, there isn't a well-funded coalition working to shape federal transportation law, as there was in the early 1990s and late 2000s.

But there is incredible new energy in the environmental movement, especially from young activists represented by groups such as the Sunrise Movement.[21] They have influenced a new generation of Congress members such as Massachusetts' Pressley and New York's Alexandria Ocasio-Cortez, who have injected climate change into the national agenda in a way I have not seen in years, under the banner of the "Green New Deal," a blueprint for rapidly decarbonizing U.S. energy, transportation, buildings, agriculture, and industry.[22] At its core is the idea that America must make its economy carbon-neutral, in ways that create well-paying jobs and repair historical oppression of marginalized communities.

Doing this with urgency (whether by passing a Green New Deal or through some other legislation) requires, among many other things, enabling cities to provide first-class bus networks. Restoring federal transit operating support and growing overall transit funds would allow every city to ramp up bus service, in places where it would be immediately popular. This one policy change would make transit a proper alternative to driving for more people and expand access to the city for everyone, especially low-income people, while also providing green jobs in the form of operator and mechanic positions.

Bus service could also be improved by fulfilling the unfunded transportation mandate of the Americans with Disabilities Act. Such a program might subsidize paratransit operations, taking

Core Federal Transportation Programs (Amounts as of Fiscal Year 2018)

Program	FY18 Amount	Stated Purpose	Can It Be Used for Transit?	Who Controls It?
Highway programs				
National Highway Performance Program	$22.38 billion	Improving the condition and performance of the National Highway System (interstates and major roads).	Yes, for bus terminals serving the National Highway System and transit capital projects in the same corridor as a limited-access highway.	State departments of transportation (DOTs).
Surface Transportation Block Grant Program[a]	$10.55 billion	Flexible program that can be used for multimodal projects.	Yes, for any transit capital project (including buying buses).	State DOTs must "suballocate" (reserve) $3.2 billion for projects selected by metropolitan planning organizations (MPOs). State DOTs control the rest but must ensure that half of overall program funding is spent in metropolitan regions.
Highway Safety Improvement Program	$2.27 billion	Improving safety for all road users.	No, but funds can be used to improve pedestrian safety on streets and intersections where transit operates.	State DOTs. States must establish a safety plan and use funds only on projects in that plan.

(Continued)

Core Federal Transportation Programs (Amounts as of Fiscal Year 2018; *Continued*)

Program	FY18 Amount	Stated Purpose	Can It Be Used for Transit?	Who Controls It?
Congestion Mitigation and Air Quality	$2.35 billion	Improving air quality in regions with high levels of air pollution.	Yes, for transit projects that can be shown to improve air quality. This includes operating costs of a new transit service.	State DOTs.
National Highway Freight Program	$1.16 billion	Improving the movement of freight on highways.	No.	State DOTs.
Transportation Alternatives Program[a]	$850 million	Projects that enhance walking. $83 million within the program is reserved for recreational trails.	Yes, for transit-priority street projects.	State DOTs suballocate $223 million to MPOs; states control the rest. Both must run a competitive process whereby local governments and other entities can apply for funds.
Railway–Highway Crossings	$235 million	Projects to improve safety where roads cross railways.	Yes, for improvements to grade crossings with rail transit.	State DOTs.

(*Continued*)

Core Federal Transportation Programs (Amounts as of Fiscal Year 2018; *Continued*)

Program	FY18 Amount	Stated Purpose	Can It Be Used for Transit?	Who Controls It?
Transit programs				
Urbanized Area Formula (secs. 5307 and 5340)	$5.1 billion	Transit capital needs in metropolitan areas. $575 million of this program can be used to cover operating costs by small transit agencies (which operate fewer than 100 vehicles).	Must be used for transit.	Transit agencies.[b]
Enhanced Mobility of Seniors and Individuals with Disabilities (sec. 5310)	$272 million	Transit capital and operating costs for services that meet the needs of seniors and people with disabilities.	55% must be used for transit; 45% can be used for other purposes, such as accessible taxis and walkability improvements.	Transit agencies receive funds in major metropolitan regions; states receive funds for rural areas and small regions.
Rural Area Formula and Transit Assistance Program (secs. 5311, 5311(b)(3), and 5340)	$673 million	Transit capital and operating costs in rural areas, except for $12.9 million reserved for training and technical assistance.	Must be used for transit.	Transit agencies; $12.9 million is split between states and the federal government for training and technical assistance.
State of Good Repair (sec. 5337)	$2.96 billion	Transit capital needs, specifically maintenance and repair of systems that are at least 7 years old.	Must be used for transit.	Transit agencies.

Core Federal Transportation Programs (Amounts as of Fiscal Year 2018; *Continued*)

Program	FY18 Amount	Stated Purpose	Can It Be Used for Transit?	Who Controls It?
Buses and Bus Facilities (sec. 5339)	$1.14 billion	Purchasing buses, building, repairing, and renovating bus maintenance facilities and passenger stations.	Must be used for transit.	$649 million goes to transit agencies by formula; $489 million goes to transit agencies through two competitive grant programs.
Capital Investment Grants (sec. 5309)	$2.62 billion	Building new fixed-guideway and rapid bus projects.	Must be used for transit.	Transit agencies apply for funding through a competitive grant program.

This table summarizes what I consider the "core" federal transportation programs, which add up to $52.6 billion.

Not including the discretionary BUILD program, the total amount of federal highway and transit funding apportioned to states and other recipients in FY2018 was $54.8 billion. That total includes several programs not listed here, including planning and research programs; programs that cover federal lands, Indian reservations, and Appalachian development projects; and $148.5 million for the Washington Metropolitan Area Transportation Authority. Also omitted is funding returned to the Federal Highway Administration (FHWA) and the Federal Transit Administration (FTA) to cover the costs of administering the programs.

FHWA programs are generally referred to by name, whereas FTA programs are often referred to by the section of federal law that defines them; I follow that convention here.

a The Transportation Alternatives Program is a set-aside within the Surface Transportation Block Grant Program (STBGP); the STBGP total is shown here after accounting for that set-aside.

b This is a bit of shorthand; FTA formula funds go to "designated recipients" that include states, counties, and regional authorities that operate transit.

Sources:

Federal Highway Administration, "Fiscal Year (FY) 2018 Supplementary Tables—Apportionments Pursuant to the Fixing America's Surface Transportation Act." March 7, 2018. https://www.fhwa.dot.gov/legsregs/directives/notices/n4510824/n4510824_t1.cfm

Federal Transit Administration, "Fiscal Year 2018 Apportionment Tables (Full Year)." July 16, 2018. https://www.transit.dot.gov/funding/apportionments/fiscal-year-2018-apportionment-tables-full-year stress off of transit agency budgets. It might fill in sidewalks, with an emphasis at bus stops and busy intersections. (Beyond bus service, it could also retrofit rail stations at older transit systems that are still inaccessible to people with disabilities.)

Many other transit provisions could be included in a Green New Deal or a federal infrastructure or transportation policy bill informed by it. But what they choose *not* to fund is as important as what they do fund. Federal policy must make it harder to build new roads, recognizing that highways are fossil fuel infrastructure as surely as oil and gas pipelines are and that their construction often directly harms neighborhoods where black and brown people live, so that suburban residents can get a faster trip.

Working for better bus service demands actions as local as placing a bench at the corner stop and as lofty as a Green New Deal. One can lead to the other. Congresswoman Pressley's political career perfectly encapsulates this. Five months before she released the ad that helped propel her into national politics, Pressley was standing with advocates at the LivableStreets Alliance, calling for bus-only lanes on Boston's streets.[23]

CONCLUSION

—

Winning Mindsets and Growing Movements

When you compare the fortunes of bus systems in different places in the United States and around the world, you begin to realize that the extended decline of bus ridership in some cities is not an inevitable consequence of changes in demographics, technologies, or consumer preferences.

It's a consequence of stasis. Many transit systems have held still while cities, markets, and technologies around them have transformed. Where people live and work is changing every year. Deliveries, transportation network companies, and an influx of high-income people to central cities together have put more vehicles on the road, worsening traffic. And thanks to the rise of Uber and Lyft, bikeshare, and scooters, there are more ways for people to get around cities than ever.

Many transit systems have held still while cities, markets, and technologies around them have transformed.

Yet in many cities, the most effective way to move the masses has stood still. Many agencies still dispatch buses using a schedule, knowing full well that active management is the only way to defeat bunching. In Washington, Los Angeles, and Chicago, the most popular bus lines in the city still crawl along in traffic, bleeding riders every year. And it is no surprise that, in the 21st century, the CEO of the Columbus transit system could look at a bus map from the 1970s and recognize the routes.

As you've read, some of this is due to indifference from decision-makers. When politicians and the transit agency board members they appoint don't value bus riders, the unspoken mission that gets transmitted to agency staff is "Don't do anything that might cause controversy; don't make anybody mad." With these marching orders, agencies can keep running service. They can improve their facilities and maps. They can buy nicer buses and develop better branding. But they can't do the things that have the most potential to make bus service more useful for many people, such as consolidating bus stops, changing routes, or giving the bus priority over cars.

And as you've also read, buses are held back through outright hostility from people with power. When lawmakers are determined to cut transit funds or willing to ban transit-only lanes or keep buses out of downtown squares, the result is austerity that keeps transit agencies struggling to plan and operate service and keeps their riders marginalized.

A bus system that doesn't change as its city changes around it is doomed to continually lose ground, like a nest egg that is kept in cash instead of being invested in a way that gains a return.

The good news is that cities can see bus gains in short periods of time. What it takes is alliances of reformers, inside and outside of government.

When you look at the regions that have done the most to improve transit, you nearly always find three kinds of champion: civic advocacy organizations, public agency managers, and elected officials.

During a particularly desperate brainstorming session, my colleagues at TransitCenter called this coalition the "hamburger of reform," with agency leaders sandwiched between civic and elected leaders. Although this metaphor seemed too silly to publish at the time, I still think about it when I see a transit reform effort that is struggling.

When you pick up a sandwich without a lower bun, the bottom drops out—and when transit agencies try to stripe bus lanes, consolidate bus stops, or redesign networks without the backing of advocates, their efforts often collapse midway through. Without the presence of pro-transit advocates, a few opponents are usually enough to dominate headlines and public meetings, scaring politicians into retreat. Elected officials can often win new funding for transit with the backing of labor and business groups. But without advocates who understand transit, this money often gets spent in ways that minimize political conflict (e.g., more buses, not more bus lanes).

Eating a sandwich without a top bun is messy and slow. Without enthusiasm from the elected officials who control budgets, so is fixing the bus. Advocates have to run repeated pressure campaigns to get the bus on the agenda and then to convince politicians to support every new bus improvement. This means reform happens in painstaking and piecemeal fashion.

The good news is that cities can see bus gains in short periods of time.

Finally, two pieces of bread without a filling is the worst sandwich of all: the dreaded nothing-burger. When public agencies are weak, reforms get watered down or bottlenecked in ways that satisfy no one. City council members earmark money for shelters, but the agency places them thoughtlessly. Advocates win a commitment to a network redesign, but the agency rolls it out poorly and behind schedule, sapping enthusiasm for more change.

A good meal needs good ingredients. And transit reform demands strong advocates, elected officials, and agency leaders. If you aspire to be one of them, here's what I believe you can learn from the change efforts in this book.

Understand Transit Systems and Power Structures

Every reformer I spoke to while writing this book had thought deeply about both transit networks (and how to plan them effectively) and the networks of power (and how to navigate them successfully). To achieve change, you have to understand both.

This begins by considering the goals of transit and what better buses are in service of. Transit agencies often deliver poor outcomes not because of incompetence by any one person but because of unclear or muddled goals. Agencies may be asked to reduce traffic congestion, increase social equity, provide service that is competitive with driving, and provide lifeline service for low-income people, all while minimizing burden to taxpayers and controversy for political officeholders. What comes out is lukewarm gruel.

When transit agencies are pulled in different directions, advocates and elected leaders can help force and direct a conversation about what transit should accomplish, by asserting the value of useful all-day bus service over rail extensions to sprawling suburbs or the importance of rapid bus lanes to the environmental sustainability of a city. They can also change the calculus around political controversy. When outside reformers are strong enough, they can create such a groundswell for bus improvements that the way to "minimize controversy" is to address their demands.

Agencies, too, should be clear about their goals and how they operationalize them, through programs such as the SFMTA's service equity strategy and Jarrett Walker's ridership–coverage exercise.[1] One of the most effective ways to talk about improving bus service is through the frame of expanded access and freedom.

Clear thinking about the goals transit is meant to accomplish should lead to clear measures of success. This unleashes transit agency staff and leaders, giving them clearer direction in how they plan and communicate with outside stakeholders. When the goal of a street is to move the most people (not the most cars), it is easier to justify transit capacity improvements. When transit is framed as a way to strengthen a neighborhood, planners can use data showing that bus corridor improvements have led to increased sales revenue for businesses.[2]

For advocates, some knowledge of transit is essential. Christof Spieler, the Houston advocate-turned-agency-board-member, said, "It's really important from an advocacy standpoint . . . to have enough technical understanding of how transit works that what you're asking for is something that you know the agency can do. If you don't understand the constraints the agency is operating under, and you make a series of asks that are not plausible, you're going to get ignored."

Understanding transit helps advocates avoid pushing for the wrong goals or goals that are unachievable. But technical knowledge also helps advocates make bolder requests, by helping them understand how much better transit can be than it is in most cities.

"Everything that we're advocating for is driven by some amount of evidence-based knowledge," said Marta Viciedo of Miami's Transit Alliance. "We're not always talking about [the data], but everything is backed up. If you go to our website, you'll see where the ideas come from."

As important as understanding transit is understanding the dynamics of power in your city. Without this understanding, it is impossible for advocates to have strategy; they are simply shouting into the wind (or their Twitter feed) and hoping someone listens.

A fundamental advocacy skill is "power mapping," diagramming which officials have the ability to enact a preferred policy, where those officials stand, and which interest groups and donors they listen to.

> *Understanding transit helps advocates avoid pushing for the wrong goals or goals that are unachievable.*

My former colleagues Kate Slevin and Jon Orcutt often talk about the importance of advocates "being in the right room"—focusing their efforts where people with influence or decisionmaking authority are present. Advocates are often invited to participate in volunteer advisory groups or rider councils. If these have access to power or inside information (for example, if transit executives or project managers regularly brief the rider council), they can be worthwhile. If not, they can take up time that would be better spent talking to reporters, organizing voters, and meeting directly with decisionmakers.

Beyond understanding a city's power dynamics, advocates need to understand how to grow and use their own power. Technical knowledge, combined with smart communications, can give advocates the power to define the problem with buses in a city and outline the solutions. Seeing the vacuum of leadership in Miami, the Transit Alliance was single-handedly able to refocus the transit conversation on buses.

Government leaders can do it as well. In Houston, Christof Spieler began talking about the need to redesign the bus network years before other agency leaders were willing to take it on. Once local politics necessitated that METRO improve buses, Spieler had a ready-made solution. This is often the case for transportation advocates: You spend time and effort articulating an agenda for change, and months or even years later, a moment of opportunity arrives to put that agenda into practice.

Developing the right relationships and organizing community members and grassroots volunteers gives advocates the power to start forcing the agenda themselves. Accomplished advocates play an "inside game," which relies on relationships with agency staff and politicians, and an "outside game," which can include media campaigns, rallies and petitions, and even electoral politics.

Advocates are most successful at building relationships when they help transit agencies do their own jobs better, for example, by providing data of the kind that LivableStreets collects through its street ambassador teams. "We're almost always coming to the table with information, resources, or a solution," executive director Stacy Thompson said. "You do that for a decade, and you can't help but be in a close relationship with the city."

Public agency staff benefit when they understand how to work with advocates to advance joint goals. Staff shouldn't expect or demand that advocates toe their agency's party line. But many a campaign has benefited from transit planners sharing their thoughts (sometimes outside of work hours, over a coffee or a beer) about which alderman is holding up a project, which internal agency data would bolster the case for a bus lane, or which agency board member is a quiet "no" vote on a low-income fare program.

Transit agency board members can be a key bridge, because they have access to agency staff and data, while having the privilege of being independent political actors. In Houston, Spieler was one of the most energetic advocates for the need to redesign the bus, first as an outside advocate but later as an agency board member, which allowed him to speak with institutional authority but maintain a voice. "One of my favorite phrases was 'I am one vote out of nine,'" Spieler said. "Board members are not spokespersons for the agency. [We're] allowed to be blunt, and that's very important. I was out there making the case for what we were about to do before the consultants were even hired."

Having said all this, not every group is equally well positioned to force its way to the table. Public agencies, foundations, and transit advocates must make more room for organizations that are led by people of color or represent marginalized communities. Metro Transit's decision to run outreach for its Better Bus Stops program through community groups led to more equitable outcomes. In Chicago, the advocacy group Active Transportation Alliance has made "mini-grants" to community groups to survey and organize riders in low-income neighborhoods.[3] Groups such as Portland's OPAL can grow and keep the lights on thanks to support from funders such as the MRG Foundation.

A Campaign Mindset

Some advocacy groups operate as watchdogs. They look out for legislative and agency actions that affect their issues and then start barking. They write a blog post analyzing the state legislature's budget. They organize against a bus service cut. They issue a press release explaining why a fare increase is inequitable.

Public agencies, foundations, and transit advocates must make more room for organizations that are led by people of color or represent marginalized communities.

That is valuable work, but it is often reactive. What most of the advocates profiled in this book do instead is *run campaigns*. They envision the outcomes they want—the city with better bus service that they want to see—and work backwards from there to figure out who has the power to make that happen and how those figures can be influenced.

"About three years ago, we decided to really shift from talking about the transit system [broadly] to just having a better buses program," Stacy Thompson of LivableStreets Alliance said. "That really made it a lot easier for us—to go from talking about these big systems to just saying, 'Okay, based on [Boston Transportation Department] data and the GoBoston 2030 plan, these are very specific corridors that [the city] needs to work on. And then we built a ground game around them."

That "ground game" meant staffing a single bus corridor with four staff members and volunteers, multiple days a week, for several weeks, a level of focus that is often not possible for advocacy groups whose mission spreads them more thinly.

Small campaigns tend to lead to larger ones. Discrete, winnable campaigns can grow an organization's confidence and credibility;

attract new volunteers, donations, and allies; and make bigger fights possible.

Inside public agencies, too, a campaign mindset breeds urgency. Cities often release transportation "action plans" outlining an agenda for improving transit. If you want to know whether one of these plans is meaningful, check whether any of the action items has a deadline that falls within the mayor's current term in office.

Agencies that take deadlines seriously broadcast them. Houston METRO held multiple media events as the clock ticked down to the launch of its redesign, according to Kurt Luhrsen, the planner who managed the process. These included press briefings 100 days and 50 days before the new network began operations. It had a communications calendar that external relations staff referred to, emphasizing different media themes to push in different weeks. And inside its headquarters and every one of its bus operating facilities, Luhrsen said, the agency installed a giant tear-off calendar counting down the days to the new network.

Get Representative, Strategic Public Input

Luhrsen said he's seen network redesign attempts fail elsewhere in the country because of poor outreach. "The first time the public has heard anything about [the redesign] is when a draft plan hits the floor," Luhrsen said. "Everybody is shocked and upset; they don't understand why this is happening. Then you spend days, weeks, months, years trying to explain yourself."

Public engagement is critical, but how agencies do it matters. Agencies often think that they have a strong public engagement strategy because they perform a lot of outreach activities. They host multiple open-door listening sessions or hold town hall meetings with elected officials. But no method of public engagement can ever reach the majority of people who will be affected by changes to bus service. Someone will always be surprised. Someone will always be opposed. Someone will always try to stop the change.

I would go as far as saying that when it comes to improving bus service, traditional public engagement, done without thought to strategy, can lead to worse outcomes than if the agency does no outreach at all.

Traditional open houses, town halls, and public hearings privilege wealthier, older, organized residents. They are often held at times that are convenient for people with 9-to-5 schedules or at times that would require someone to take time off work; they are often advertised through channels that only the connected know about, such as an elected official's mailing list. They bring out the people with the strongest opinions, not the majority of residents. Ten angry people at a town hall can cause journalists and politicians to perceive a groundswell against a project, even if those ten are the only people in the neighborhood with strong feelings.

No method of public engagement can ever reach the majority of people who will be affected by changes to bus service.

I'm often asked, by agency staff or advocates, "What message can win over project opponents? What framing will stop them from criticizing our bus lane and calling their elected officials?" The reality is that winning over the most implacable opponents is impossible without fatally compromising the project. And so the point of public outreach cannot be that every "community concern" will be addressed and assuaged. That does nothing but give the loudest people a heckler's veto.

Instead, I believe public engagement needs to achieve two goals. First, it should get input that is representative of the people who will benefit from better bus service, best achieved through surveying at bus stops, tabling at community events, and other methods that bring the agency to community members instead of the other way around. Because bus riders' voices are so often ignored, there is nearly always unmet demand for better buses in a city. Before Metro Transit started its Better Bus Stops program, there was plenty of demand for shelters. Before Houston METRO redesigned its bus routes, there were plenty of people who wanted them to be better. Representative public outreach documents this demand and helps public agencies wield a popular mandate for buses.

Second, it must be strategic. Just as advocates draw "power maps" of who can influence a desired policy, agency staff need a keen sense of the stakeholders who have the power to champion or derail their project—such as employers, anchor institutions, major nonprofits, and advocates—and engage them early. METRO's redesign project brought in more than a hundred stakeholders before a single new bus route was drawn.

"We had a lot of the tough conversations before we even started to design [the new network]," METRO's Kurt Luhrsen said. Although stakeholders might have disagreed about specific bus routes, he said, "We all agreed that the system was broken and something needed to happen. That became very important [later on] when there was opposition, that the board could go back and say, 'this is what we as a community, we as a board said was important.'"

A smart communication strategy, which draws on thoughtful data to explain the social benefits of transit, helps skeptics keep an open mind, like the store owner who sees statistics showing that sales revenues increased around the last rapid bus corridor the city opened. It excites pro-transit advocates and elected officials and gives them strong talking points they can use in their own efforts. It also creates new supporters, such as the chamber of commerce that didn't realize how much a network redesign could expand the labor pool. It sets bus improvements up to succeed, even when the politics are naturally stacked against them.

Build Agencies That Can Deliver

Dynamic transit agency leadership is important to steer reform. But the structure and strength of bureaucracies matter as well. Once there's a strong political consensus that better buses are needed, the important question increasingly becomes whether the agency can deliver. Reformers need to start turning their attention to how an agency's structure, capacity, processes, and metrics affect its ability to deliver better transit.

This might mean updating an agency's street design manual, or the metrics it uses to judge a project's success. It might mean hiring a dedicated "transit team," as the Boston Transportation Department did in 2019. It might mean reorganizing a transportation agency to give bus priority projects a clear home, creating a speed and reliability unit like the kind that exists at King County Metro, or hiring more outreach staffers and dispatchers. All of these help create a new, transit-supportive status quo at public agencies and ensure that future administrations can't easily undo the hard work of reform.

Transit researcher Simon Berrebi said teams like King County Metro's speed and reliability unit are a rare breed: "At many agencies, you have an empty planning department across the street from a building full of consultants."

But that in-house approach is what enables King County Metro to work in so many places. Its speed and reliability team develops and maintains a web of relationships, learning about slowdowns on the street from bus operators and working with municipal engineers to make spot fixes. It is a continuous improvement machine that could not function if it had to rely on consultants hired for each separate project.

Advocates need to understand the granular details of how public agencies work, too. "[We] are obsessed with the City of Boston's hiring process," Stacy Thompson of LivableStreets said. "We want to understand who they're hiring, what the roles are, and what is the process for project deployment. We get in the weeds; I know we sometimes annoy them. But unless you care about it at that level, you're going to keep getting one-off projects."

Finally, transportation leaders can help themselves by improving basic agency functions, such as HR and procurement, that often get in the way of trying to do things quickly.

Grow a Stronger Transit Reform Movement

Cities would be better off with more and stronger transit advocates. Miami's Transit Alliance shows how much a single advocacy group can do in a city that previously had none. And the results in Boston and Seattle demonstrate what is possible when cities have thriving advocacy ecosystems. To win better buses in more cities, we need more wonky transit blogs, more faith-based organizing, more riders' unions, and more state budget watchdogs.

We also need more ways for transit reformers in one city to learn from the triumphs and pitfalls of others. This already happens on an occasional basis, as when Austin's Capital Metro invited transit planners from Baltimore and Houston to share lessons from their bus network redesign efforts. Advocates, too, share stories. Stacy

Thompson, the LivableStreets Alliance executive director, said that at least once a month she fields calls from transit groups elsewhere in the country asking for advice.

TransitCenter, the foundation I've worked at, has organized learning networks for transit advocates and for agency staff and board members. The National Association of City Transportation Officials helps city staff meet and trade best practices through its conferences and other events. More formal, resourced networks would help turn ad hoc relationships into something more.

We need more ways for transit reformers in one city to learn from the triumphs and pitfalls of others.

"In my dream world, we have the capacity to do more trainings—or to go beyond that," Thompson said. "LivableStreets is something that could happen nationally; it's so easily replicable. If I had money and had flexibility, I'd want to devote more time to a national movement."

The fastest way to grow the transit reform movement is for local foundations to show sustained interest and energy. Energetic volunteers can do it for a time, but they'll inevitably burn out. During Transit Alliance's first 6 months, Azhar Chougle and Marta Viciedo ran full-time businesses while essentially working full-time as unpaid co-directors. That kind of volunteerism can't keep an organization running forever.

Philanthropists who want to change transit for the better need to stay committed. Many foundations look for catalytic moments, awarding grants to advocates when the political opportunity seems ripe and scaling back support once the moment has passed, so that funds can be redeployed to some new cause. That logic is understandable, but it starves movements.

It is true that reforms cannot occur until the right political opportunity arrives, but they will never occur if reformers are not prepared to seize the opportunity. Advocates need to be strong enough in the fallow years to build power and develop a clear agenda. That strength allows them to be effective when the moment arrives and also helps them create new opportunities on their own. If foundations pull their support after advocates win, they can kill momentum just as advocates have the opportunity to reach for more. Almost any advocate who has had to rely on foundation dollars can tell a story about how boom-and-bust fundraising has thrown their organization into chaos.

Foundations often backfill government functions, including public transportation. In Cincinnati, the Haile Foundation contributes $900,000 annually toward the operating budget of the underperforming Bell Connector streetcar—a sum that could transform transit in the city if it stood up an advocacy group instead.[4] The National Committee for Responsive Philanthropy has found that, across policy areas, the average dollar invested in advocacy results in $115 in social benefit.[5] Transportation is no exception, when you consider the millions of dollars in revenue won by advocates in Indianapolis or the expanded opportunities won for young Portlanders thanks to OPAL's work.

During my time at TransitCenter, I've seen how much transit advocates have been able to accomplish with even small, short-term grants. But it is local, place-based foundations such as Boston's Barr Foundation (a supporter of LivableStreets Alliance) and the Miami Foundation (which supports Transit Alliance) that have the capability to grow advocacy over the long haul. Every foundation that cares about climate change, wealth inequality, and social inclusion should be investing in the people working for more sustainable and equitable public transit.

Unleashing the Bus

Every so often, when I'm reading or watching a piece of popular culture from outside the United States, I'll notice a bus. But I'm not sure non–transportation planners would. That's because, in foreign media, the bus is nearly always unremarkable.

In the Hong Kong film *Tempting Heart*, the lovers at the center of the story take buses often, including to a hotel where they sleep together for the first time.[6] In the Canadian graphic novel series *Scott Pilgrim*, the bus is the setting for the meet-cute between Scott and his girlfriend, Knives Chau, who drops a stack of books that Scott is all too happy to pick up.[7] In Haruki Murakami's short story

"Cream," the protagonist gets off the train in Kobe, Japan, transferring to a bus that winds up a hilly path that he thinks will take him to a piano concert.[8] In the BBC thriller *Killing Eve*, an MI5 security operative impulsively punches through the glass at a bus shelter, perhaps a reflection of her inner turmoil.[9]

In these scenes, the bus carries little of the class symbolism that it does in American culture. The bus system fades into the background because, like a park or sidewalk, it is simply part of the city. It's a means for lovers, concertgoers, and intelligence agents alike to get around town. With the bus as a backdrop, we can focus on the stories that actually matter in these characters' lives.

What is so tragic about the stories we read about buses and the people who ride them in America is that they are so often stories of dreams deferred: the student who can't get to night school, the patient who can't access healthcare, the families whose opportunities are foreclosed upon.

There isn't much that is "sexy" about improving the bus, just as there is little that is flashy about fixing streetlights or sewers. But better streetlamps lead to fewer people dying in traffic.[10] Safe, lead-free pipes help children grow to realize their full potential.

Similarly, the particulars of better buses can sometimes feel granular, or technical, or bureaucratic. But each step to improve bus service represents a meaningful improvement in the lives of hundreds of people who wait at a particular bus stop, or the thousands who use a specific bus route, or the hundreds of thousands who ride the bus in a given city.

Each step to improve bus service represents a meaningful improvement in the lives of hundreds of people who wait at a particular bus stop.

That's why I find the stories of better bus service fought for and won to be so meaningful. It is heartening to witness the growing number of places in the United States where local leaders are fighting to unleash the potential of bus service. As the many success stories in this book show, your city has the power to join them.

NOTES

—

Introduction

1. Xavier Lassiter, "3-Hour Commute Includes 3 Buses, 1 Train." *New Haven Independent*, September 17, 2014. https://www.newhavenindependent.org/index.php/ archives/entry/three_hour_commute_includes_three _buses_and_a_train/

2. Ratasha Smith, "Lost, Looking for the J Bus." *New Haven Independent*, December 3, 2014. https://www .newhavenindependent.org/index.php/archives/entry/lost _in_the_hamden_hills_looking_for_the_j_bus/

3. Jodie Mozdzer Gil, "Brenda Works Around the F Bus." *New Haven Independent*, September 22, 2014. https://www .newhavenindependent.org/index.php/archives/entry/ brenda_durdens_f_bus_workaround/

4. "Hella Blows." *Insecure*. HBO. August 27, 2017.

5. "Working Girls." *Broad City*. Comedy Central. February 5, 2014.

6. "The Big Bang." *Atlanta*. FX. September 6, 2016.

7. American Public Transportation Association, Public Transportation Ridership Reports, Fourth Quarter 2008 and Fourth Quarter 2018. https://www.apta.com/ wp-content/uploads/Resources/resources/statistics/ Documents/Ridership/2008_q4_ridership_APTA.pdf and https://www.apta.com/wp-content/uploads/2018-Q4 -Ridership-APTA.pdf.

8. Bryan Blanc et al., "Effect of Urban Fabric Changes on Real Estate Property Tax Revenue: Evidence from Six American Cities." *Transportation Research Record* 2453 (2014): 145–152.

9. Richard Rothstein, *The Color of Law*. New York: Liveright, 2017: 126–131.

10. William H. Frey, "US Population Disperses to Suburbs, Exurbs, Rural Areas, and 'Middle of the Country' Metros." *The Avenue (Brookings Institute)*, March 26, 2018. https://www.brookings.edu/blog/the-avenue/2018/03/26/us-population-disperses-to-suburbs-exurbs-rural-areas-and-middle-of-the-country-metros/

11. Lara Fishbane, Joseph Kane, and Adie Tomer, "Stop Trying to Solve Traffic and Start Building Great Places." Brookings Institution, March 20, 2019. https://www.brookings.edu/blog/the-avenue/2019/03/20/stop-trying-to-solve-traffic-and-start-building-great-places/

12. Reid Ewing et al., "Does Urban Sprawl Hold Down Upward Mobility?" *Landscape and Urban Planning* 148 (April 2016): 80–88. https://doi.org/10.1016/j.landurbplan.2015.11.012

13. Marlon Boarnet et al., "First/Last Mile Transit Access as an Equity Planning Issue." *Transportation Research Part A: Policy and Practice* 103 (September 2017): 296–310.

14. Kelcie Ralph and Evan Iacobucci, "Driven to Participate (Literally): Transportation Barriers to Teen Activity Participation." Presentation at the 97th Annual Meeting of the Transportation Research Board, Washington, DC, January 2018.

15. "Whose Streets?" *On the Media*, WNYC, New York, November 23, 2018.

16. Nicholas J. Klein and Michael J. Smart, "Car Today, Gone Tomorrow: The Ephemeral Car in Low-Income, Immigrant and Minority Families." *Transportation* 44 (2017): 495. https://doi.org/10.1007/s11116-015-9664-4

17. R. J. Cross et al., "Driving into Debt: The Hidden Costs of Risky Auto Loans to Consumers and Our Communities." Frontier Group and U.S. Public Interest Research Group, February 13, 2019. https://frontiergroup.org/reports/fg/driving-debt

18. U.S. Environmental Protection Agency, "Inventory of U.S. Greenhouse Gas Emissions and Sinks, 1990–2016." https://

www.epa.gov/ghgemissions/inventory-us-greenhouse-gas
-emissions-and-sinks

19. International Energy Agency, "Energy Efficiency Indica-
tors 2018: Highlights." December 7, 2018. https://webstore
.iea.org/energy-efficiency-indicators-2018-highlights

20. Andrew J. Hawkins, "The Boring Company's Chicago
Project Seems Awfully Cheap for Something So Big." *The
Verge*, June 14, 2018. https://www.theverge.com/2018/6/14/
17464612/boring-company-chicago-elon-musk-cost-estimate

21. Bruce Schaller, "The New Automobility: Lyft, Uber and
the Future of American Cities." Schaller Consulting,
July 25, 2018. http://www.schallerconsult.com/rideservices/
automobility.pdf

22. Yves Smith, "Uber Is Headed for a Crash." *New York*,
December 4, 2018. http://nymag.com/intelligencer/2018/12/
will-uber-survive-the-next-decade.html

23. California Air Resources Board, "2018 Progress Report:
California's Sustainable Communities and Climate Protection Act." November 2018. https://ww2.arb.ca.gov/sites/
default/files/2018-11/Final2018Report_SB150_112618_02
_Report.pdf

24. John Larsen et al., "Transcending Oil: Hawaii's Path to a
Clean Energy Economy." Rhodium Group, April 19, 2018.
https://rhg.com/research/transcending-oil-hawaiis-path-to
-a-clean-energy-economy/

25. Project Drawdown, "Sector Summary: Transport." https://
www.drawdown.org/solutions/transport. Accessed January 31, 2019.

26. Matthew Yglesias. "Get On the Bus." *Slate*, August 7, 2013.
https://slate.com/technology/2013/08/bus-rapid-transit
-improved-buses-are-the-best-route-to-better-transit.html

27. Matt McFarland, "Cities Realize They Must Fix the Sorry
State of Buses." CNNMoney, October 27, 2017. https://
money.cnn.com/2017/10/27/technology/business/city-buses/
index.html

28. Laura Bliss, "Love the Bus, Save Your City." *CityLab*,
May 7, 2018. https://www.citylab.com/transportation/2018/
05/love-the-bus-save-your-city/559262/

Chapter 1: What Makes People Choose the Bus?

1. Jon Hilkevitch, "New CTA Boss Dorval Carter Jr.'s View: Faster Buses, Quieter Riders on Phone." *Chicago Tribune*, June 14, 2015. http://www.chicagotribune.com/ news/columnists/ct-cta-president-getting-around-met0615 -20150614-column.html

2. David Crowley and Brandon Hemily, "Profiling Transit Ridership." Strategic Transit Research Program Synthesis, Canadian Urban Transit Association, November 2000.

3. Edward A. Beimborn, Michael J. Greenwald, and Jia Xia, "Transit Accessibility and Connectivity Impacts on Transit Choice and Captivity." Center for Urban Transportation Studies and Department of Urban Planning, University of Wisconsin–Milwaukee, Transportation Research Board, 2003.

4. Gregory Thompson, Jeffrey Brown, Torsha Bhattacharya, and Michal Jaroszynski, "Understanding Transit Ridership Demand for a Multi-Destination, Multimodal Transit Network in an American Metropolitan Area, Research Report 11-06." Mineta Transportation Institute Publications, 2012.

5. Katherine Gregor, "10 Reasons to Love a Streetcar." *Austin Chronicle*, July 20, 2007. http://www.austinchronicle.com/ news/2007-07-20/505120/

6. Ralph Buehler and John Pucher, "Demand for Public Transport in Germany and the USA: An Analysis of Rider Characteristics." *Transport Reviews* 32, no. 5 (September 2012): 541–567. https://nhts.ornl.gov/2009/pub/ demandforpublictransport.pdf

7. Los Angeles Metro, "On-Board Survey Results + Trend Report Fall '17." http://media.metro.net/projects_studies/ research/images/infographics/2017_fall_onboard_survey _results.pdf

8. For King County, see King County Metro Transit. "2016 Rider Survey Report." March 2017. https://kingcounty .gov/~/media/depts/transportation/metro/accountability/ reports/2016/2016-rider-survey-final.pdf. For New York,

see NuStats, "2008 New York Customer Travel Survey: Final Report." August 2009. http://web.mta.info/mta/planning/data/NYC-Travel-Survey/NYCTravelSurvey.pdf

9. Joe DeLessio, "Governor Cuomo Says the MTA's New Wi-Fi-Equipped Buses Will Have 'Almost a Ferrari-Like Look.'" *New York Magazine*, March 8, 2016. http://nymag.com/intelligencer/2016/03/mtas-new-buses-will-have-wi-fi.html

10. Adella Santos et al., "Summary of Travel Trends: 2009 National Household Travel Survey." https://nhts.ornl.gov/2009/pub/stt.pdf

11. Daniel Kay Hertz, "Undercounting the Transit Constituency." *City Observatory*, February 23, 2016. http://cityobservatory.org/undercounting-the-transit-constituency-2/

12. Michael Manville et al., "Falling Transit Ridership: California and Southern California." Southern California Association of Governments, January 2018. https://www.scag.ca.gov/Documents/ITS_SCAG_Transit_Ridership.pdf

13. Douglas Hanks, "With Metrorail So Costly, Mayor Touts a Miami Commuting on High-Tech Buses." *Miami Herald*, November 1, 2017. https://www.miamiherald.com/news/local/community/miami-dade/article182190971.html

14. Douglas Hanks, "As Transit Ridership Drops, Miami-Dade Wants to Cut Bus Stops and Outsource Routes." *Miami Herald*, May 5, 2017. https://www.miamiherald.com/news/local/community/miami-dade/article148954014.html

15. Transit Alliance, "Where's My Bus?" https://transitalliance.miami/campaigns/where-s-my-bus/ridership

16. Transit Alliance, "Mobility Scorecard." https://transitalliance.miami/campaigns/mobility-scorecard

Chapter 2: Make the Bus Frequent

1. Steven Higashide and Zak Accuardi, "Who's On Board 2016: What Today's Riders Teach Us about Transit That Works." TransitCenter, 2016; Steven Higashide and Mary

Buchanan, "Who's On Board 2019: How to Win Back America's Transit Riders." TransitCenter, February 2019.

2. Los Angeles Metro. "NextGen Bus Study: Transit Competitiveness and Market Potential," November 2018. http://media.metro.net/about_us/committees/images/presentation-tac-ngs.pdf

3. Jarrett Walker, *Human Transit*. Washington, DC: Island Press, 2011: 117–134.

4. Houston METRO. "Stakeholder Task Force Kick Off Meeting Presentation." May 29, 2013. https://ridemetro.granicus.com/MetaViewer.php?view_id=5&clip_id=604&meta_id=8474

5. Torrey Lyons, Reid Ewing, and Guang Tian, "Coverage vs. Frequency: Is Spatial Coverage or Temporal Frequency More Impactful on Transit Ridership?" Utah Department of Transportation, November 2017. http://mrc.cap.utah.edu/wp-content/uploads/sites/8/2015/12/Coverage-vs-Frequency.pdf

6. Ryan Holeywell, "These Charts Show Poverty's Startling Spread Across Houston." Kinder Institute Research, November 14, 2016. https://kinder.rice.edu/2016/11/14/these-charts-show-how-povertys-startling-spread-across-houston

7. Kurt Luhrsen, "Reimagining Houston's Local Bus Network" (slide 4). Presentation at APTA Bus and Paratransit Conference, May 2016. https://www.apta.com/mc/bus/previous/2016bus/presentations/Presentations/Luhrsen-Kurt.pdf

8. Miya Shay, "METRO Accused of Violating Federal Law." ABC13. https://abc13.com/archive/7656465/

9. Mike Morris, "Metro in a Quandary as Transit Funding Heads to Voters." *Houston Chronicle*, April 27, 2012. https://www.chron.com/news/houston-texas/article/Metro-in-a-quandary-as-transit-funding-heads-to-3513987.php

10. Houston METRO, Agenda, August 30, 2012 board meeting. https://ridemetro.granicus.com/MetaViewer.php?view_id=5&clip_id=413&meta_id=21192

11. Houston METRO, "Request for Qualifications (RFQ) no. RFQ1200013 Transit System Re-Imagining Project."

September 27, 2012. https://ridemetro.granicus.com/
MetaViewer.php?view_id=5&clip_id=432&meta_id=21301

12. Houston METRO, "Project Update: Presentation to
the Stakeholder Task Force." December 2013. https://
ridemetro.granicus.com/MetaViewer.php?view_id=5&clip
_id=738&meta_id=8350

13. Houston METRO, "December 2018 Monthly Ridership Report." https://www.ridemetro.org/Pages/
RidershipReport-122018.aspx

14. Daniel Vock, "Buses, Yes Buses, Are 'The Hottest Trend
in Transit.'" *Governing*, September 2017. https://www
.governing.com/topics/transportation-infrastructure/gov
-big-city-bus-systems.html

15. TransitCenter, "How Austin's Capital Metro Pulled Off a
Bus Network Redesign." July 25, 2018. http://transitcenter
.org/2018/07/25/austins-capital-metro-pulled-off-bus
-network-redesign/

16. Mark Robinson, "Richmond City Council Approves
$747 Million Budget with New Cigarette Tax." *Richmond
Times-Dispatch*, May 13, 2019. https://www.richmond
.com/news/local/city-of-richmond/richmond-city-council
-approves-million-budget-with-new-cigarette-tax/article
_2c768727-fb70-5671-bb58-1bf9b277387b.html

17. Mid-Ohio Regional Planning Commission, "2016–2040
Columbus Area Metropolitan Transportation Plan"
(Chapter 6). May 2016. http://www.morpc.org/wp-content/
uploads/2017/12/000MTP_Report_Chapter6.pdf

18. Investing in Place et al., "Re: NextGen Bus Study." Letter
to Los Angeles Metro board. March 20, 2019. https://
investinginplace.org/wp-content/uploads/2019/03/2019-03
-20-Letter-to-Metro-on-NextGen-Bus-Study.pdf

19. Jarrett Walker, "The Bus Is Still Best." *The Atlantic*,
October 31, 2018. https://www.theatlantic.com/technology/
archive/2018/10/bus-best-public-transit-cities/574399/

Chapter 3: Make the Bus Fast and Reliable

1. For the statistic on a penguin, see Pete Donohue, "Buses Ain't Up to Speed: Pokier Than a Penguin Crosstown." *New York Daily News*, November 13, 2003. For the statistic on a sprinting rat, see Bus Turnaround Coalition, "Half of All NYC Bus Routes Get a 'D' for Speed and Reliability." March 6, 2019. http://busturnaround.nyc/get_involved/half-of-all-nyc-bus-routes-get-a-d-for-speed-and-reliability/

2. Kate Hinds (@katehinds). May 27, 2018. https://twitter.com/katehinds/status/1000869513791930370

3. Arlene Weintraub, "An Unhealthy Commute." Center for an Urban Future, January 2018.

4. *Transit Capacity and Quality of Service Manual*, 3rd ed. Washington, DC: National Academies Press, 2013. https://www.nap.edu/read/24766/chapter/7

5. San Francisco Municipal Transportation Authority, "All-Door Boarding Evaluation Final Report." December 2014. https://www.sfmta.com/sites/default/files/agendaitems/2014/12-2-14%20Item%2014%20All%20Door%20Boarding%20Report.pdf

6. National Association of City Transportation Officials. "Pavement Markings & Color." https://nacto.org/publication/transit-street-design-guide/transit-lanes-transitways/lane-elements/pavement-markings-color/

7. New York City Department of Transportation, "Green Means Go: Transit Signal Priority in NYC." January 2018. http://www.nyc.gov/html/brt/downloads/pdf/brt-transit-signal-priority-july2017.pdf

8. TransitCenter, Video interview with Scott Kubly, 2017. https://vimeo.com/208486810

9. NYC Bus Turnaround, "Report Cards." http://busturnaround.nyc/report-cards/, accessed March 24, 2019.

10. King County Metro, "King County Metro RapidRide Performance Evaluation Report." December 2014. http://metro.kingcounty.gov/am/reports/2014/rapidride-performance-evaluation-report-2014.pdf

11. Max Smith, "Regionwide Bus Route Overhaul to Start
     Next Year." WTOP, January 25, 2019. https://wtop.com/dc
     -transit/2019/01/region-wide-bus-route-overhaul-to-start
     -next-year/

12. New York City Department of Transportation, "New
     York City Mobility Report." June 2018. http://www.nyc
     .gov/html/dot/downloads/pdf/mobility-report-2018-screen
     -optimized.pdf

13. Jarrett Walker + Associates, "Philadelphia Bus Network
     Choices Report." June 2018. http://www.septa.org/service/
     bus/network/pdf/2018-philadelphia-choices-report-chapter
     -2.pdf

14. Author's calculation using TransitCenter's Transit Insights
     tool, which visualizes National Transit Database trends.
     http://insights.transitcenter.org/

15. Patrick Sisson, "How Your Online Shopping Snarls Traf-
     fic on City Streets." *Curbed*, January 10, 2019. https://www
     .curbed.com/2019/1/10/18177399/amazon-delivery-traffic
     -online-shopping-e-commerce

16. Tom McKone, Ellen Partridge, and Jeanette Martin,
     "Eliminating Bus Bunching: Building a Process, Informa-
     tion Source, and Tool Box for Improving Service." Civic
     Consulting Alliance, 2015. https://www.ccachicago.org/wp
     -content/uploads/2015/08/tom_mckone_eliminating_bus
     _bunching.pdf

17. Institute for Transportation and Development Policy,
     "The Bus Rapid Transit Standard." June 21, 2016. https://
     www.itdp.org/library/standards-and-guides/the-bus-rapid
     -transit-standard/

18. Benno Martens, "Cleveland's Mayor Is Keeping Buses Out
     of Public Square." Citylab, February 1, 2017. https://www
     .citylab.com/equity/2017/02/clevelands-mayor-is-keeping
     -buses-out-of-public-square/515124/

19. Grant Segall, "Consultant Calls RTA Bus Service
     Efficient and Overstrained." *The Plain Dealer*, Feb-
     ruary 20, 2019. https://www.cleveland.com/metro/
     2019/02/consultant-calls-rta-bus-service-efficient-and
     -overstrained.html

20. Angie Schmitt, "Richmond Shows How to Boost Small-City Transit." *Streetsblog USA*, January 7, 2019. https://usa.streetsblog.org/2019/01/07/richmond-shows-how-to-boost-transit-ridership-in-a-smaller-city/

21. Steven Higashide, "Express Trains to O'Hare Are Nice, but Let's Get Back on the Bus." *Chicago Sun-Times*, June 14, 2018. https://chicago.suntimes.com/columnists/ohare-express-train-transit-in-chicagons/

22. Massachusetts Department of Transportation, "City of Everett, MBTA: Broadway Bus Lane Pilot Program." December 8, 2016. https://blog.mass.gov/transportation/uncategorized/city-of-everett-mbta-broadway-bus-lane-pilot-program/

23. Ned Oliver, "VDOT Will Oversee Construction of GRTC's Pulse." *Richmond Times-Dispatch*, October 26, 2015. https://www.richmond.com/news/local/city-of-richmond/vdot-will-oversee-construction-of-grtc-s-pulse/article_3cbd208b-ae73-5efc-9aeb-a0ff60c583c0.html

24. TransitCenter, "Everett Bus Lane: The Little Pop-Up That Could." January 2, 2018. http://transitcenter.org/2018/01/02/everett-bus-lane-the-little-pop-up-that-could/

25. "Massachusetts Avenue Bus Priority Pilot." Presentation on November 14, 2018. https://www.arlingtonma.gov/home/showdocument?id=44642

26. Elise Harmon, "How Can We Fix This? How MAPC's Data Helped Boston Make a Bus Line Faster." Metropolitan Area Planning Council, June 8, 2018. https://www.mapc.org/planning101/how-can-we-fix-this-how-mapcs-data-helped-boston-make-a-bus-line-faster/

27. City of Boston, "Permanent Bus Lane to Be Established on Washington Street in Roslindale." June 7, 2018. https://www.boston.gov/news/permanent-bus-lane-be-established-washington-street-roslindale

28. WalkUP Roslindale, "WalkUP Comment Letter on Washington Street Bus Lane." October 7, 2018. http://www.walkuproslindale.org/weblog/2018/10/07/walkup-comment-letter-on-washington-street-bus-lane/

29. Coalition for Smarter Growth webpage, https://www
.smartergrowth.net/, accessed February 25, 2019.
30. Frederick Kunkle, "Is It RIP for WMATARU? WMATA
Riders Union Seems as Dysfunctional as Metro Right
Now." *Washington Post*, April 21, 2016. https://www
.washingtonpost.com/news/tripping/wp/2016/04/21/
is-it-rip-for-wmataru-wmata-riders-union-seems
-as-dysfunctional-as-metro-right-now/?utm_term=
.b3eab70495b1
31. Angie Schmitt, "Downtown Seattle Added 45,000 Jobs and
Hardly Any Car Commuters." *Streetsblog USA*, February 10,
2017. https://usa.streetsblog.org/2017/02/10/downtown
-seattle-added-45000-jobs-and-hardly-any-car-commuters/
32. King County, "Service Partnerships." https://www
.kingcounty.gov/transportation/kcdot/MetroTransit/
TransitNow/Partnerships.aspx
33. Seattle Department of Transportation, "Bridging the Gap:
Annual Report 2015." https://www.seattle.gov/Documents/
Departments/SDOT/About/BTG/BTG_Annual_Report
_2015.pdf
34. City of Seattle, "Seattle Department of Transportation
Organizational Chart." September 2017. http://www
.seattle.gov/documents/Departments/SDOT/About/SDOT
_OrgChart.pdf
35. City of Seattle, "Seattle Department of Transportation Organizational Chart." March 2019. https://www
.seattle.gov/Documents/Departments/SDOT/About/
SDOTOrgChartQ32018.pdf
36. King County Metro, "Transit Speed and Reliability Guidelines and Strategies." March 2017. https://kingcounty.gov/
~/media/depts/transportation/metro/about/planning/speed
-reliability-toolbox.pdf
37. Sarah Maslin Nir, "As Subway Crisis Takes Up 'So
Much Oxygen,' the Buses Drag Along." *New York Times*,
March 8, 2018. https://www.nytimes.com/2018/03/08/
nyregion/new-york-city-bus-troubles.html
38. For Everett, see Bruce Mohl, "Bus Lane: Everett Just
Did It." *Commonwealth Magazine*, September 17, 2018.

https://commonwealthmagazine.org/transportation/bus
-lane-everett-just-did-it/. For Somerville, see Joseph Cur-
tatone, "Investing in Bus Service Is an Investment in Our
Future." *Somerville Times*, March 1, 2019. https://www
.thesomervilletimes.com/archives/89851

39. Adam Vaccaro, "More Bus Lanes Are Coming to Boston."
Boston Globe, March 7, 2019. https://www.bostonglobe
.com/metro/2019/03/07/more-bus-lanes-are-coming
-boston/qFMghGlK6h2CRlzBdOI2EM/story.html

40. City of Boston, "Join Us in Transforming Boston's Transportation System." September 7, 2018. https://www.boston
.gov/news/join-us-transforming-bostons-transportation
-system

Chapter 4: Make the Bus Walkable and Dignified

1. Sarah Goodyear, "When Design Kills: The Criminal-
ization of Walking." *Grist*, July 21, 2011. https://grist
.org/infrastructure/2011-07-20-when-design-kills-the
-criminalization-of-walking/

2. Los Angeles Department of Transportation, "Vision
Zero Los Angeles: The Facts." 2015. Accessed at http://
visionzero.lacity.org/wp-content/uploads/2015/08/LA
_VisionZero_FactSheet.pdf

3. Los Angeles Metro, "On-Board Survey Results + Trend
Report Fall '17." http://media.metro.net/projects_studies/
research/images/infographics/2017_fall_onboard_survey
_results.pdf

4. Danielle Furfaro, "Fuming Residents Say Staten Island Bus
Route Revamp Is a Disaster." *New York Post*, September 26,
2018. https://nypost.com/2018/09/26/fuming-residents-say
-staten-island-bus-route-revamp-is-a-disaster/

5. TransitCenter, "How Austin's Capital Metro Pulled Off a
Bus Network Redesign." July 25, 2018. http://transitcenter
.org/2018/07/25/austins-capital-metro-pulled-off-bus
-network-redesign/

6. A fully built-out sidewalk network in Austin would
be 4,980 miles; see City of Austin, "Sidewalk Master

Plan/ADA Transition Update." June 16, 2016. https://
austintexas.gov/sites/default/files/files/Public_Works/
Street_%26_Bridge/Sidewalk_MPU_Adopted_06.16
.2016_reduced.pdf. As of April 2019, there are 2,100 miles
of missing sidewalk; in other words, roughly 42 percent
of the sidewalk network is incomplete; see City of Austin,
"Austin Strategic Mobility Plan," Chapter 3. April 11,
2019. http://www.austintexas.gov/sites/default/files/files/
Transportation/ASMP/ASMP_Chapters/AdoptedASMP
_Chapter3_Supply_Reduced.pdf

7. Ja Young Kim, Keith Bartholomew, and Reid Ewing,
"Impacts of Bus Stop Improvements." Sponsored by Utah
Department of Transportation, March 2018. http://mrc.cap
.utah.edu/wp-content/uploads/sites/8/2015/12/UT-18.04
-Impacts-of-Bus-Stop-Improvements.pdf

8. Angie Schmitt, "Seattle Tosses Out Rulebook to Protect
Pedestrians." *Streetsblog USA*, February 5, 2019. https://usa
.streetsblog.org/2019/02/05/seattle-tosses-out-the-rulebook
-to-protect-pedestrians/

9. Angie Schmitt, "How Engineering Standards for Cars
Endanger People Crossing the Street." *Streetsblog USA*,
March 3, 2017. https://usa.streetsblog.org/2017/03/03/how
-engineering-standards-for-cars-endanger-people-crossing
-the-street/

10. Denver Moves: Pedestrians and Trails. https://www
.denvergov.org/content/denvergov/en/denveright/
pedestrians-trails.html

11. Mike Morris, "Houston Struggles to Expand Sidewalk
Efforts." *Houston Chronicle*, December 19 2018. https://
www.houstonchronicle.com/news/houston-texas/houston/
article/Houston-struggles-to-expand-sidewalk-efforts
-13487583.php

12. TriMet, "Improving Pedestrian Access to Transit." 2012.
Accessed February 6, 2019 at https://trimet.org/walk/

13. Meg Gatto, "RTA Wants to Build Transit Hub in Downtown New Orleans." Fox 8, April 16, 2014. http://www
.fox8live.com/story/25257572/rta-wants-to-build-transit
-hub-in-downtown-new-orleand/

14. Nick Swartswell, "Transit Activists Place Benches at Cincinnati Bus Stops." *CityBeat*, June 13, 2018. https://www.citybeat.com/news/blog/21009110/transit-activists-place-benches-at-cincinnati-bus-stops

15. Carolina A. Miranda, "Meet the Anonymous Artist Installing Bus Benches at Neglected Stops on L.A.'s Eastside." *Los Angeles Times*, November 28, 2018. https://www.latimes.com/entertainment/arts/miranda/la-et-cam-anonymous-bus-bench-artist-20181128-story.html

16. Yingling Fan, Andrew Guthrie, and David Levinson. "Perception of Waiting Time at Transit Stops and Stations." Center for Transportation Studies, University of Minnesota, 2016. Retrieved from the University of Minnesota Digital Conservancy, http://hdl.handle.net/11299/180134

17. Mary Buchanan and Kirk Hovenkotter, "From Sorry to Superb: Everything You Need to Know about Great Bus Stops." TransitCenter, 2018.

18. Salt Lake City Council, "Bus Shelter Advertising Common Practices." December 2013. http://www.slccouncil.com/agendas/2013Agendas/Dec03/120313A16.pdf

19. Dan Rivoli, "Jumaane Williams, Lt. Gov. Candidate, Gets Busload of Criticism over New Route." *New York Daily News*, September 4, 2018.

20. Los Angeles Office of the City Controller. "Audit of the City's Street Furniture Contract with CBS Decaux, LLC." January 12, 2012. https://www.scribd.com/document/311169518/Bus-Shelter-Audit

21. Brian Lamb, "Fulfilling Our Commitment to Creating a Better Bus Stop." Metro Transit *Riders' Almanac* blog. February 27, 2018. https://www.metrotransit.org/fulfilling-our-commitment-to-creating-a-better-bus-stop

22. Eric Roper, "Hundreds of Metro Bus Stops Have Thousands Seeking Shelters." *Star-Tribune*, September 25, 2014. http://www.startribune.com/july-7-hundreds-of-metro-bus-stops-have-thousands-seeking-shelters/265979041/

23. Metropolitan Council of the Twin Cities, "Choice, Place and Opportunity: An Equity Assessment of the Twin Cities." https://metrocouncil.org/Planning/Projects/Thrive

-2040/Choice-Place-and-Opportunity/FHEA/Choice,
-Place-and-Opportunity-Executive-Summary.aspx

24. Berry Farrington and Caitlin Schwartz, "Better Bus Stops
Community Engagement Report." May 2017. https://www
.metrotransit.org/Data/Sites/1/media/about/improvements/
betterbusstopscommunityengagementreport.pdf

25. Metro Transit, "Better Bus Stops: Shelter Placement
Guidelines." January 2018. https://www.metrotransit.org/
Data/Sites/1/media/about/improvements/06-115-01-18_bbs
-placement-guidelines.pdf

26. Berry Farrington, "Data (Actually!) Changed Shelter
Priorities, Practice and Policy." Presentation at APTA
Multimodal & Sustainability Workshop, July 31, 2018.

27. Texas Department of Transportation, "2019–2022 Statewide Transportation Improvement Program: Highway
Projects." http://ftp.dot.state.tx.us/pub/txdot-info/tpp/stip/
2019-2022/highway.pdf

28. Jon Murray, "I-70 Overhaul: What You Need to Know
as Denver's First Major Freeway Project in More Than
a Decade Starts This Week." *Denver Post*, July 29, 2018.
https://www.denverpost.com/2018/07/29/i-70-construction
-project-denver-transportation-central-70/

29. For a "standard-size" shelter, according to transit officials
in Cleveland, Detroit, Louisville, and Columbus, see Angie
Schmitt, "We Should Put a Shelter at Every Bus Stop in
America," *Streetsblog USA*, October 1, 2018. https://usa
.streetsblog.org/2018/10/01/opinion-we-should-put-a-bus
-shelter-at-every-stop-in-america/

30. Author's calculation using the 2017 National Transit Database tables "Service" and "Capital Expenses."

31. Atlanta Regional Commission, "ARC to Receive $3.8
Million in State Funding to Support Regional Bus Stop
Signage Upgrades." June 27, 2016. https://atlantaregional
.org/news/press-releases/arc-to-receive-3-8-million-in-state
-funding-to-support-regional-bus-stop-signage-upgrades/

32. Better Bus Coalition, "Bus Shelter Locations—An Equity
Issue." December 17, 2018. https://betterbuscoalition.org/
blog/2018/12/17/bus-shelter-locations-an-equity-issue

33. Angie Henderson District 34 Councilwoman, "Walkable
     Neighborhoods." July 23, 2015. https://www.angieforcouncil
     .org/neighborhoods/walkable-neighborhoods/

34. Joey Garrison, "Nashville to Require More Developers
     Provide Sidewalks." *The Tennessean*, April 18 2017. https://
     www.tennessean.com/story/news/2017/04/18/nashville
     -require-more-developers-provide-sidewalks/100597870/

35. Janne Flisrand, "Rider Requests for Better Bus Stops."
     Streets.MN, August 10 2016. https://streets.mn/2016/08/10/
     rider-requests-for-better-bus-stops/

36. Community Engagement Team, "Better Bus Stops
     Community Engagement Report | Appendix A: Bet-
     ter Bus Stops Community Engagement Team Final
     Report." Metro Transit, April 2017. https://www
     .metrotransit.org/Data/Sites/1/media/about/improvements/
     betterbusstopscommunityengagementreport.pdf

Chapter 5: Make the Bus Fair and Welcoming

1. Zak Accuardi, "Title VI Is Broken. Here's How Transit
     Leaders Can Fix It." *Next City*, October 26, 2018. https://
     nextcity.org/daily/entry/title-vi-is-broken-heres-how
     -transit-leaders-can-fix-it

2. Derek Thompson, "How Hollywood Accounting Can
    Make a $450 Million Movie 'Unprofitable.'" *The Atlantic*,
    September 14, 2011. https://www.theatlantic.com/business/
    archive/2011/09/how-hollywood-accounting-can-make-a
    -450-million-movie-unprofitable/245134/

3. Alex Karner and Aaron Golub, "Comparison of Two
    Common Approaches to Public Transit Service Equity
    Evaluation." *Transportation Research Record: Journal of the
    Transportation Research Board* 2531 (January 2015): 170–179.

4. Steven Higashide and Hayley Richardson, "Transit Equity
    Starts at Home, Not in Washington." *Governing*, July 31
    2018. http://www.governing.com/gov-institute/voices/col
    -transit-equity-fairness-title-VI.html

5. San Francisco Municipal Transportation Authority, "Muni
    Service Equity Strategy FY 2019 and FY 2020." https://

www.sfmta.com/sites/default/files/reports-and-documents/
2018/03/2018_muni_service_equity_strategy_report
_power_point_presentation_0.pdf

6. Eric Roper, "Met Council's Equity Push Hard to See on the Ground." *Star-Tribune*, May 12, 2018. http://www.startribune.com/met-council-s-equity-push-hard-to-see-on-the-ground/482459011/

7. Jon Collins, "Race, Poverty Tied to Metro Transportation Funding." Minnesota Public Radio, September 18, 2014. https://www.mprnews.org/story/2014/09/18/race-poverty-transportation-funding

8. Conan Cheung, "Where Have All the Riders Gone?" November 8, 2017. Presentation at 2017 California Transit Association conference. https://caltransit.org/cta/assets/Fall%20Conference/2017/PPTs/Fiscal%20Planning%20Policy%20Compliance/FISCAL-Where%20Have%20All%20the%20Riders%20Gone-Cheung(1).pdf

9. Candice Williams, "Detroit Union: More Cops Equal Fewer Transit Assaults." *Detroit News*, June 16, 2016. https://www.detroitnews.com/story/news/local/detroit-city/2016/06/14/police-detroit-buses-people-mover/85895924/

10. Graham Currie et al., "Perceptions and Realities of Personal Safety on Public Transport for Young People in Melbourne." World Transit Research, 2010. https://www.worldtransitresearch.info/research/3823/

11. National Academies of Sciences, Engineering, and Medicine. *Transit Security Update*. Washington, DC: The National Academies Press, 2008. http://nap.edu/23058

12. Steven Higashide and Mary Buchanan, "Who's On Board 2019." TransitCenter. http://transitcenter.org/publications/whos-on-board-2019/.

13. Anastasia Loukaitou-Sideris and Camille Fink, "Addressing Women's Fear of Victimization in Transportation Settings." *Urban Affairs Review* 4, no. 4 (2008): 554–587.

14. "The Universe of Transit Safety." TransitCenter, March 27, 2018. http://transitcenter.org/2018/03/27/universe-transit-safety/

15. Yingling Fan, Andrew Guthrie, and David Levinson, "Perception of Waiting Time at Transit Stops and Stations." Center for Transportation Studies, University of Minnesota, 2016. Retrieved from the University of Minnesota Digital Conservancy, http://hdl.handle.net/11299/180134

16. Sarah Kaufman, Christopher Polack, and Gloria Campbell, "The Pink Tax on Transportation: Women's Challenges in Mobility." NYU Rudin Center for Transportation. https://wagner.nyu.edu/impact/research/publications/pink-tax-transportation-womens-challenges-mobility

17. Heather Redfern, "Transit Facility Center Gives Help, Hope to Those 'With Nowhere to Go.'" *Metro Magazine*, April 17, 2018. https://www.metro-magazine.com/blogpost/729382/hope-for-helping-the-homeless

18. Q. David Bowers, *The History of United States Coinage as Illustrated by the Garrett Collection*. Bowers and Ruddy Galleries, 1979.

19. Jon Hilkevitch, "CTA's Ventra Debit Option Rife with Fees." *Chicago Tribune*, March 20, 2013. https://www.chicagotribune.com/news/ct-xpm-2013-03-20-ct-met-cta-ventra-hidden-fees-0320-20130320-story.html

20. SEPTA, "Reminder: Transfers Available Only on SEPTA Key Card Starting Aug. 1." July 24, 2018. http://www.septa.org/media/releases/2018/7-24-18.html

21. Todd Litman, "Transit Price Elasticities and Cross-Elasticities." Victoria Transport Policy Institute, November 27, 2018.

22. Alexis F. Perotta, "Transit Fare Affordability: Findings from a Qualitative Study." *Public Works Management & Policy* 22, no. 3 (May 24, 2016).

23. Kirk Johnson, "Targeting Inequality, This Time on Public Transit." *New York Times*, February 28, 2015. https://www.nytimes.com/2015/03/01/us/targeting-inequality-this-time-on-public-transit.html

24. Ameena Walker, "Half-Price MetroCard Program Launches, but Only to 30K New Yorkers." *Curbed*,

January 4, 2019. https://ny.curbed.com/2019/1/4/18168604/
mta-fair-fares-program-launch

25. Youth Environmental Justice Alliance and OPAL, "Youth-
    pass to the Future." April 2016. http://www.opalpdx.org/
    wp-content/uploads/2016/04/YouthTransitReport-online
    .pdf

26. Michael J. Smart and Nicholas J. Klein, "Remem-
    brance of Cars and Buses Past: How Prior Life
    Experiences Influence Travel." *Journal of Planning
    Education and Research* 38, no. 2 (June 2018): 139–151.
    doi:10.1177/0739456X17695774

27. "Thousands of Bus Riders Don't Pay, and Most Get Away
    with It." WFMY, June 26, 2017. https://www.wfmynews2
    .com/article/news/local/2-wants-to-know/thousands-of-bus
    -riders-dont-pay-and-most-get-away-with-it/452229126

28. Vin Barone, "Transit Chief Wants to Fight Bus Fare
    Evasion with More Cops." *AM New York*, March 26,
    2019. https://www.amny.com/transit/mta-fare-evasion-1
    .28962852

29. Alexa Delbosc and Graham Currie, "Four Types of Fare
    Evasion: A Qualitative Study from Melbourne, Austra-
    lia." *Transportation Research Part F: Traffic Psychology and
    Behaviour* 43 (November 2016): 254–264. https://doi.org/10
    .1016/j.trf.2016.09.022

30. Vicki Lancaster and Aaron Schroeder, "A Study of Metro-
    bus Fare Evasion." Presentation to WMATA, July 25,
    2017. https://www.bi.vt.edu/content/generic/WMATA-fare
    -evasion-data-analysis-presentation.pdf

31. Mitch Ryals, "D.C. Council Overrides Mayor Muriel
    Bowser's Veto of Metro Fare Evasion Decriminaliza-
    tion." *Washington City Paper*, January 22, 2019. https://
    www.washingtoncitypaper.com/news/loose-lips/article/
    21044376/dc-council-overrides-mayor-muriel-bowsers
    -veto-of-metro-fare-evasion-decriminalization

32. Angie Schmitt, "The Case for Decriminalizing Fare
    Evasion." *Streetsblog USA*, February 22, 2018. https://usa
    .streetsblog.org/2018/02/22/the-case-for-decriminalizing
    -fare-evasion/

33. Andrew Theen, "Immigrant, Advocate, Daughter: Kathy
     Wai, TriMet's Youngest-Ever Board Member, Shakes
     Things Up." *The Oregonian*, November 21, 2018. https://
     www.oregonlive.com/news/2018/11/immigrant-advocate
     -daughter-kathy-wai-trimets-youngest-ever-board
     -member-shakes-things-up.html
34. *City of Cleveland v. Ronnie Williams* 2017 CRB 015467.
     Cleveland Municipal Court. October 26, 2017.

Chapter 6: Gerrymandering the Bus

1. Henry Grabar, "Can America's Worst Transit System Be
    Saved?" *Slate*, June 7 2016. https://slate.com/business/2016/
    06/detroit-has-americas-worst-transit-system-could-the
    -regional-transit-master-plan-save-it.html
2. Paige Williams, "Drop Dead, Detroit!" *The New Yorker*,
    January 27, 2014. https://www.newyorker.com/magazine/
    2014/01/27/drop-dead-detroit
3. Angie Schmitt, "How Structural Racism at Regional
    Planning Agencies Hurts Cities." *Streetsblog USA*, Jan-
    uary 5, 2018. https://usa.streetsblog.org/2018/01/05/how
    -structural-racism-at-regional-planning-agencies-hurts
    -cities/
4. Chas Sisk, "New Amp Deal Would Give State Veto Power
    on BRT Projects." *The Tennessean*, April 17, 2014. https://
    www.tennessean.com/story/news/politics/2014/04/17/
    lawmakers-reach-deal-amp/7825799/
5. Hayleigh Columbo, "1 in 5 Indianapolis Residents Lives in
    Poverty. And Many Areas Are Getting Worse." *Indianap-
    olis Business Journal*, May 11, 2018. https://www.ibj.com/
    articles/68785-in-5-indianapolis-residents-lives-in-poverty
    -and-many-areas-are-getting-worse
6. Sam Klemet, "IndyCan Calls For Lawmakers to Pass
    Regional Transit Plan." WFYI, November 7, 2013. https://
    www.wfyi.org/news/articles/indycan-calls-for-lawmakers
    -to-pass-regional-transit-plan
7. "Mass Transit Group Pushes Plan." Associated Press,
    November 20, 2013. https://www.southbendtribune.com/

news/politics/mass-transit-group-pushes-plan/article
_d12b2ed4-4ac6-11e3-9c2c-0019bb30f31a.html

8. "IndyCan—Guided Discussion Questions for STA."
St. Thomas Aquinas Church and School, May 17, 2014.
http://www.staindy.org/church/indycan-guided-discussion
-questions-sta/

9. Tanya Snyder, "Indiana Transit Bill Moves Forward with
Only Some of Its Worst Provisions." *Streetsblog USA,*
February 13, 2014. https://usa.streetsblog.org/2014/02/13/
indiana-transit-bill-moves-forward-with-only-some-of-its
-worst-provisions/

10. IndyGo, "Background & Public Involvement." https://
www.indygo.net/transitplan/background-public
-involvement/. Accessed March 14, 2019.

11. Indy Connect, "Marion County Transit Plan: Your
Input, Your Transit." https://indyconnect.org/wp
-content/uploads/2017/01/Marion-County-Transit-Plan
-Presentation-2015-05-13.pdf

12. Faith in Indiana, "Want Mass Movement? The Messenger
Matters!" http://www.coriecommunications.com/assets/
freelance-writing-design-photography-indycan-voter
-report.pdf

13. Dan Levine, Stephen Lee Davis, and Tia Vice, "Fight
For Your Ride: An Advocate's Guide to Improving and
Expanding Transit." February 2018, Transportation for
America.

14. Peter Simek, "Bombshell Report Reveals DART's
System-Wide Inadequacy." *D Magazine*, October 23,
2017. https://www.dmagazine.com/frontburner/
2017/10/bombshell-report-reveals-darts-system-wide
-inadequacy/

15. Dallas Area Rapid Transit, "DART Board Bylaws." As
amended September 22, 2015. https://www.dart.org/about/
board/DARTBoardBylaws.pdf

16. Dallas Area Rapid Transit, "Proposed August 2019
Service Changes and Transit System Plan Meetings."
https://www.dart.org/meetings/2019servicechange/
DARTAugust2019ServiceChange.pdf

17. Joey Garrison, "Analysis | 6 Reasons Why the Nashville Transit Referendum Lost Big." *Tennessean*, May 2, 2018. https://www.tennessean.com/story/news/2018/05/02/nashville-transit-referendum-6-reasons-why-lost-big/571782002/

18. Faith in Indiana, "Want Mass Movement? The Messenger Matters!" http://www.coriecommunications.com/assets/freelance-writing-design-photography-indycan-voter-report.pdf

Chapter 7: Technology Won't Kill the Bus—Unless We Let It

1.   Jamie McGee, "Swope Offers Another Nashville Transit Plan: Autonomous Vehicles, Stacked Interstates." *The Tennessean,* April 10 2018. https://www.tennessean.com/story/news/2018/04/10/councilman-swopes-nashville-transit-stacked-interstates/500574002/

2.   Joey Garrison, "Nashville Transit Referendum: 6 Reasons Why It Lost Big." *The Tennessean*, May 2 2018. https://www.tennessean.com/story/news/2018/05/02/nashville-transit-referendum-6-reasons-why-lost-big/571782002/

3.   Bryan Salesky, "A Decade after DARPA: Our View on the State of the Art in Self-Driving Cars." *Medium*, October 16, 2017. https://medium.com/self-driven/a-decade-after-darpa-our-view-on-the-state-of-the-art-in-self-driving-cars-3e8698e6afe8

4.   Aarian Marshall, "After Peak Hype, Self-Driving Cars Face the Trough of Disillusionment." *WIRED*, December 29, 2017. https://www.wired.com/story/self-driving-cars-challenges/

5.   Shara Tibken, "Waymo CEO: Autonomous Cars Won't Ever Be Able to Drive in All Conditions." CNET, November 13, 2018. https://www.cnet.com/news/alphabet-google-waymo-ceo-john-krafcik-autonomous-cars-wont-ever-be-able-to-drive-in-all-conditions/

6.   The Digit Group, "The Digit Group Plays Key Role in Nashville Transit Proposal Centered around Autonomous

Vehicles and Double-Decker Highways" (press release). Accessed February 11, 2019 at https://docs.wixstatic.com/ ugd/feb19d_cbf20b35c1334ee39ab4eedbd113b2c8.pdf

7. Randal O'Toole, "Transit Death Watch: April Ridership Declines 2.3 Percent." *Cato at Liberty*, June 7 2018. https:// www.cato.org/blog/transit-death-watch-23-decline-april

8. John Urgo, "Flex v. Fixed: An Experiment in On-Demand Transit." TransitCenter, May 15, 2018. http://transitcenter .org/2018/05/15/adding-flexible-routes-improve-fixed -route-network/

9. Jarrett Walker, "The Bus Is Still Best." *The Atlantic*, October 31, 2018. https://www.theatlantic.com/technology/ archive/2018/10/bus-best-public-transit-cities/574399/

10. Eric Jaffe, "The Real Benefits of Real-Time Transit Data." *Sidewalk Talk*, June 15, 2018. https://medium.com/sidewalk -talk/the-real-benefits-of-real-time-transit-data-1fee19988b73

11. Jason Lee, "SFMTA's Experiment with Real-Time Information." TransitCenter, June 7, 2018. http://transitcenter .org/2018/06/07/real-time-info-affect-transit-ridership/

12. New York City Department of Transportation, "Bus Forward." 2017. https://www1.nyc.gov/html/brt/downloads/ pdf/bus-forward.pdf

13. Alameda–Contra Costa Transit District, "Headway-Based Scheduling Opportunities." February 14, 2018. http://www .actransit.org/wp-content/uploads/board_memos/18-004 %20Headway-based%20Scheduling.pdf

14. Zak Accuardi et al., "The Data Transit Riders Want." TransitCenter and Rocky Mountain Institute, December 2018. http://transitcenter.org/wp-content/uploads/2018/12/ TC_TransitData_Final_FullLayout_121718.pdf

15. Daniel Salazar, "Lots of Driverless Buses with Dedicated Lanes: How Capital Metro Sees Austin's Public Transit Future." *Austin Business Journal*, October 3, 2018. https:// www.bizjournals.com/austin/news/2018/10/03/lots-of -driverless-buses-with-dedicated-lanes-how.html

16. Alon Levy, "Flagging Down Driverless Buses." *The American Prospect*, May 24, 2018. https://prospect.org/article/ flagging-down-driverless-buses

17. To get a good sense of the complexity of a bus operator's job, you can read the 101-page Greater Cleveland Regional Transit Authority Bus Operators' Handbook at https://uploads-ssl.webflow.com/5b853741ce0232c3d2ea46cb/5b897d0c3c6e24ff8418970b_2018%20Bus%20Operators%20Handbook.pdf

18. Christina Van Zelst, "'Humanity at Its Best:' MCTS Bus Driver Helps Baby Found Wandering Alone on Freeway Overpass." Fox 6 News, January 10, 2019. https://fox6now.com/2019/01/10/mcts-bus-driver-helps-baby-boy-found-wandering-alone-on-freeway-overpass/

19. Daniel Sperling et al., *Three Revolutions: Steering Automated, Shared, and Electric Vehicles to a Better Future*. Washington, DC: Island Press, 2018.

Chapter 8: Building a Transit Nation

1. "The 1 Bus—Ayanna Pressley for Congress." Campaign advertisement, August 7, 2018. https://www.youtube.com/watch?v=TgF79Shc_YI

2. Ayanna Pressley for Congress, "Equity Agenda for the 7th District." Accessed February 15, 2019 at https://ayannapressley.com/issues/equity-agenda/

3. See, for example, U.S. Public Interest Research Group, "Highway Boondoggles 4: Big Projects. Bigger Price Tags. Limited Benefits." June 26, 2018. https://uspirg.org/reports/usp/highway-boondoggles-4

4. Christof Spieler (@christofspieler), February 13, 2019. https://twitter.com/christofspieler/status/1095876265700179968

5. Federal Highway Administration, "Transferability of Apportioned Funds between Programs Questions & Answers." April 22, 2016. https://www.fhwa.dot.gov/cfo/transferability_qa.cfm

6. Greater Ohio Policy Center, "Fueling Innovation: Sustainable Funding for Transit in Ohio." https://www.greaterohio.org/fueling-innovation

7. Ohio Department of Transportation, "Kasich's Plan Will Invest $3 Billion in Ohio's Transportation System." Press

release, July 22, 2013. http://www.dot.state.oh.us/districts/
D05/newsreleases/Pages/TRAC.aspx

8. Don Pickrell, "Federal Operating Assistance for Urban
Mass Transit: Assessing a Decade of Experience." *Transportation Research Record* 1078 (1986). http://onlinepubs.trb
.org/Onlinepubs/trr/1986/1078/1078-001.pdf

9. Jeffrey Brown, "Paying for Transit in an Era of Federal
Policy Change." *Journal of Public Transportation* 8, no. 3
(2005). https://www.nctr.usf.edu/jpt/pdf/JPT%208-3
%20Brown.pdf

10. Brad Dicken, "Transit Routes Slashed: Only 2 to Remain."
The Chronicle, January 12, 2010. http://www.chroniclet
.com/news/2010/01/12/Transit-routes-slashed-Only-2-to
-remain.html

11. David Epstein, "Fed to Mass Transit: Drop Dead." *Salon*,
June 22, 2009. https://www.salon.com/2009/06/22/transit/

12. American Public Transit Association, "Impacts of the
Recession on Public Transportation Agencies: 2011
Update." August 2011. https://www.apta.com/resources/
reportsandpublications/Documents/Impacts-of-Recession
-August-2011.pdf

13. Heritage Foundation, "The Budget Book: 106 Ways to
Reduce the Size and Scope of Government." March 2015.
http://budgetbook.heritage.org/

14. CQ Almanac, "Surface Transportation Bill Enacted." 2012.
https://library.cqpress.com/cqalmanac/document.php?id=
cqal12-1531-87298-2553318

15. Jeff Davis, "FY19 Budget Request: Mass Transit Again
Faces 'New Start' Cuts." https://www.enotrans.org/article/
fy19-budget-request-mass-transit-faces-new-start-cuts/

16. Chuck Schumer, "No Deal on Infrastructure without
Addressing Climate Change." *Washington Post*, December 6, 2018. https://www.washingtonpost.com/opinions/
chuck-schumer-mr-president-lets-make-a-deal/2018/12/
06/aeae0188-f99e-11e8-8c9a-860ce2a8148f_story.html?utm
_term=.1620358290b8

17. Senate Democrats. "Senate Democrats' Jobs & Infrastructure Plan for America's Workers." March 7, 2018.

https://www.democrats.senate.gov/imo/media/doc/
Senate%20Democrats'%20Jobs%20and%20Infrastructure
%20Plan.pdf

18. Emma Foehringer Merchant, "A Look at the Passenger
     Transportation Challenge for the US." *GreenTech Media*,
     January 1, 2019. https://www.greentechmedia.com/articles/
     read/the-u-s-s-passenger-transportation-challenge

19. National Academies of Sciences, Engineering, and Med-
     icine, *Renewing the National Commitment to the Interstate
     Highway System: A Foundation for the Future*. Washington,
     DC: The National Academies Press, 2018. https://doi.org/
     10.17226/25334

20. Richard F. Weingroff, "Creating a Landmark: The Inter-
     modal Surface Transportation Act of 1991." *Public Roads*
     65, no. 3 (November/December 2001). https://www.fhwa
     .dot.gov/publications/publicroads/01novdec/istea.cfm

21. Emily Witt, "The Optimistic Activists for a Green New
     Deal: Inside the Youth-Led Singing Sunrise Movement."
     The New Yorker, December 23, 2018.

22. Jon Allsop, "Green New Deal Drives Sustained, but
     Shallow, Climate Coverage." *Columbia Journalism Review*,
     March 6, 2019. https://www.cjr.org/the_media_today/
     green-new-deal-coverage.php

23. Karen Morales, "Group Seeks to Prioritize MBTA Bus
     Transit." *Bay State Banner*, March 15, 2018. https://www
     .baystatebanner.com/2018/03/15/group-seeks-to-prioritize
     -mbta-bus-transit/

Conclusion

1. Jarrett Walker, "Purpose-Driven Public Transport: Creat-
    ing a Clear Conversation about Public Transport Goals."
    Journal of Transport Geography 16, no. 6 (November 2008):
    436–442.

2. National Association of City Transportation Officials,
    "Making Transit Count: Performance Measures That
    Move Transit Projects Forward." 2018. https://nacto.org/
    tsdg/making-transit-count/

3. Active Transportation Alliance, "Our Bus Advocacy Grants Are Being Put to Work!" July 12, 2018. http:// activetrans.org/blog/our-bus-advocacy-grants-are-being -put-work

4. Cedric Rose, "Tracking Cincinnati Streetcar's Success." *Cincinnati Magazine*, December 8, 2017. https://www .cincinnatimagazine.com/citywiseblog/tracking-cincinnati -streetcars-success/

5. Lisa Ranghelli, "Leveraging Limited Dollars: How Grantmakers Achieve Tangible Results." National Committee on Responsive Philanthropy, 2012. http:// bjn9t2lhlni2dhd5hvym7llj-wpengine.netdna-ssl.com/wp -content/uploads/2012/01/LeveragingLimitedDollars.pdf

6. Sylvia Chang, "Tempting Heart." Directed by Sylvia Chang. Hong Kong, 1999.

7. Bryan Lee O'Malley, *Scott Pilgrim's Precious Little Life*. Portland, OR: Oni Press, 2004.

8. Haruki Murakami, "Cream." *The New Yorker*, January 28, 2019.

9. "I Have a Thing about Bathrooms." *Killing Eve*. BBC America. May 6, 2018.

10. Todd Scott, "Detroit Public Lighting Improvements Reducing Pedestrian Fatalities." Detroit Greenways Coalition, July 16, 2018. http://detroitgreenways.org/ detroit-public-lighting-improvements-reducing-pedestrian -fatalities/